SOCCOLOGY
Inside the Hearts and Minds of Successful Professionals

Kevin George

Second Edition

Published in the United Kingdom in Paperback by:
OWN IT! Entertainment Ltd

Company Registration Number: 09154978

Copyright © 2018 Kevin George
Kevin George has asserted his right under the Copyright, Designs and Patents Act 1988 to be identified as the author of this work.

Cover illustration and design: James Nunn

Paperback ISBN: 9781916052352

All rights reserved. No part of this publication may be reproduced, stored in a retrieval system, or transmitted in any form or by any means, electronic, mechanical. photocopying, recording or otherwise, without the prior permission of the copyright owners.

WWW.OWNIT.LONDON

"An informed and entertaining insight into the footballer's multi-faceted mind"

FourFourTwo Magazine

"*Soccology* gives players a much deeper understanding of the game and educates those who care for players on how to better teach, manage and support them."

Akala, rapper, poet, former West Ham Utd Player

"A must read that gets to the heart of a game the world loves!"

Colin Kazim-Richards,
Corinthians and Turkish international

"Kevin delivered *Soccology* to our players. The players were fully engaged, and staff commented afterwards that he should run more programmes for our players, which isn't the reaction we always get from staff"

Matt Henly, Head of Education, Arsenal Football Club

"The perfect football guide! This book will change how people experience and behave in football"

Bradley Wright-Phillips, New York Redbulls

This book is dedicated to two amazing ladies

My daughter, Storm-Aurora George, who is my new motivation.

My mother, Louvine George, who is always there no matter what. Your selflessness is to be admired. You taught me from birth that I could be anything, that I should never settle and that I should always have fun. You are the reason for everything I have achieved. It's thanks to you that my life is rich in experiences.

I love you both so much.

CONTENTS

Introduction	7
State	9
Unconscious Competence	25
Mind, Body and Eyes	43
Culture	61
Mental Health	83
Leadership	113
Player Premium	137
Football Relationships	163
Off-Field Decision-Making	185
The Power of Environment	205
Acknowledgements	233
About the Author	235

INTRODUCTION

Kevin George – The Soccologist

Football is the most popular sport on the planet. Over half the world's population claim to be fans, which means that between 3.5 and 4 billion people consider soccer an important part of their lives. The sport is also big business. The total revenue of the 'Big Five' top European soccer leagues has steadily increased year on year and in 2017 was estimated at over 14 billion euros. The top 20 players in the world each earn over £10 million a year. It's hardly surprising so many kids dream of making it in football.

But the pressures of being a professional player are enormous, not just physically but emotionally. For every household name bringing home the big pay cheques there are hundreds of thousands of others who are struggling to make it, or who have been forced out because of health issues, or because their style of play or their attitude doesn't fit with the current regime. Even those who are successful can have trouble adjusting to fame, status and the expectations of everyone around them. There are many issues in football that are just not being addressed.

I've experienced football on the streets of south London, in the Sunday league, professionally and on screen as a sports model. I played for Charlton Athletic FC and West Ham United FC, featured in Sky One's *Dream Team* as Durant

Thomas, body doubled for Cristiano Ronaldo, Thierry Henry, John Abrahams and more. My varied relationships with football have allowed me to experience the game from different angles.

Studying Neuro-Linguistic Programming, counselling and psychotherapy has helped me to understand the behaviour of those in football and to bring the physical activity and the emotional experience together. As a human performance consultant, I deliver development programmes across the Premier League, from the Under-10s to the first team as well as staff and parents.

My studies sparked my curiosity. I researched the game further, looking at everything from the intelligence of footballers and concerns about their wellbeing to how culture affects football and how parents can best support their kids. This resulted in the creation of the Soccology service, offering psycho-emotional support to players, parents and staff.

On my travels around football clubs, I found the same problems were showing up and being repeated across generations. I knew this was important and that I needed to share what I have learnt with a wider audience, which is why I wrote this book. It's for anyone who wants to have the best experience playing football and who aspires to be the greatest version of themselves.

In every chapter you'll get an insight into the hearts and minds of professional footballers from the world's top leagues. Players past, present and upcoming, as well as a coach, a manager and a psychophysicist have talked to me about areas of their lives that they've never shared before. They explain how they have developed and utilised their thinking skills to gain an advantage and discuss their feelings, and how thoughts and emotions affect performance. Welcome to the world of Soccology.

ONE

STATE

In the field of coaches, a deep understanding of the human psyche is required to put the right person in the right place.
—Johan Cruyff

Think of a time when you had the lowest amount of energy you've ever experienced. Take a moment to remember the situation and revisit it in your mind's eye. What can you see and hear around you? Is it in colour or black and white? What can you smell or taste? Once you can vividly imagine this, give your energy level a number from one to ten, (with one the lowest and ten the highest). Can you think of a word to describe how you feel?

Look out! A roaring lion is racing towards you, saliva flying from its gaping jaws as it hurtles closer and closer. Quick, do something or you're going to be the lion's lunch! Do you run? Do you hide? Using the same scale of one to ten, what number would you give your energy levels now? And what word would you use to describe how you feel? I'm guessing there's a big difference in both.

You have just experienced a change of state, in this case, moving from low and lethargic to alert and powered up. It's something that takes place in training grounds and stadiums across the globe every day. Managers have the power to change players' states in a heartbeat. They can drain their emotional energy with criticism and negativity. Or, like the lion in the room, they can get players energised and highly motivated. I want to take a closer look at state, because the effect that the mind has on performance is so important.

Claudio Ranieri was good for me and he was happy to give me my break and play me, and over time his confidence in me grew.

He used to call me a Rottweiler. I remember we had a game against Charlton in the league and he was going through the names of the players. When he got to midfield he said 'Gronkjaer, Lampard,' and instead of saying 'Nicolas' he said 'Rottweiler'. Everyone was in absolute hysterics because of his accent and his use of the nickname. Looking back now, it was a clever psychological move. I think the reason he did it was take the pressure off me as a youngster in the team, trying to solidify a career and prove I deserved to be there. It took pressure off the team as a whole because the game was an important one we had to win to remain in the Premier League title race. The whole atmosphere in the changing room changed with that one joke.

When Jose Mourinho took over at Chelsea, I was worried like most young players when they are on the fringe and the manager gets sacked. We all know if the incoming manager doesn't favour you, you can't move to another Premier League team like the more established players, so the only way is down. I felt vulnerable, a young squad player who had been given a chance by Ranieri. That was until I learnt that Mourinho knew everything about me, including how many appearances I'd made. I thought wow! It was reassuring and impressive. He made me feel as though I was important to him before he had decided whether I was important to him. He won me over from day one. Other managers were not doing that. He was different, and he set the bar.

Two things that really impressed me about Mourinho: on the first day we trained, we did a keep ball square and he absolutely blasted one of his assistant managers in front of the players. At the time I was shocked but looking back it was a clever move because you think, 'There are no favourites here. If he thinks someone's wrong he will tell them they're wrong, whether they're his assistant or not.' At other clubs it's never like that because coaches are never wrong.

Secondly, we had a pre-season game against Oxford United FC and he knew every detail about their players. This is a man that had just won the biggest competition with Porto, the Champions League, and now the manager of Chelsea and he took the time to do thorough research for a pre-season game of a team that were leagues below us. By doing so, he gave us no reason to not do well. He also made us familiar with situations we would come up against. Our minds were reassured which allowed our physical talents to shine through.

—**Alexis Nicolas**
former Chelsea and Cyprus international

The state you're in

Your 'state' is the condition you are in at a specific time: your way of being, your mood and your feelings, arising from your physiology, thinking and emotions. The main way we experience and interpret the world around us is through our state. It can cause us to feel motivated or depressed, and everything in between.

State is being acknowledged more in football through youth module courses and the use of sports psychologists. Both are playing a key role in pushing the game in a more mindful direction, but there are question marks over whether they're going into enough detail. Although the focus is usually on the player, an understanding of state is as important for trainers and managers. I believe that an emotionally sound person has a positive impact on the player; providing a positive place to filter experience improve outcomes and allows them to express themselves in a different way.

Players and managers may still not be familiar with the concept of state, but unconsciously they rely on it heavily. They talk about getting 'into the zone' and do different things to get into a resourceful state. To get game-ready some use music, others have their own personal superstitions and rituals. As a team, players often shout, 'Come on aye lads!' before they leave the changing room, which is followed by intense breathing, pawing and a double jump.

Throughout my 20-year involvement in professional football, I have seen and experienced three performance states that Neuro-Linguistic Programming recognises:

- **Unresourceful State (URS):** This has a negative and detrimental effect on a performance, a career or a life. People in this state may demonstrate anger, loss of confidence, anxiety or limiting beliefs. In football, URS can place invisible shackles on a player, leading them to take simple options, think twice about an action and leave them spiritually drained. URS also has an impact on the performance of management and coaching staff, affecting their decisions, tactics and communication.
- **Resourceful State (RS):** When in a resourceful state, a person operates using calculated and chosen responses. They have a tranquil inner space to access when needed. Being able to visit this place develops an awareness of choice, an ability to reflect and emotional intelligence. These skills, which are the building blocks of confidence, self-esteem and self-belief, are the basis of a fruitful performance, career and life. Coaching staff control the climate in which they coach and how they manage themselves. A coach that operates in a resourceful state for the majority of the time gives his players a comfortable foundation to build upon and is also, perhaps unknowingly, a role model in state management.

    Unresourceful states and resourceful states are a unique part of our identity, but they're not only experienced by individuals. They are also felt by groups of people who act 'as one', such as football teams. An example of this is the so-

called 'twelfth man' advantage when a team plays at home. It's not just the physical familiarity of the home ground, it's the power of the fans cheering them on which powers up the players to such an extent that they feel as though they have an extra player on the field. On the flipside, if the team are not doing well, then the home advantage can become a disadvantage if the fans are unhappy and booing every move. Under those circumstances, the thought of an away game can seem like a welcome relief.
- **High Performing State (HPS):** In football, this state is known as being 'in the zone'. Players are unconsciously powered, playing in the moment on autopilot. Mihály Csikszentmihályi refers to HPS as 'flow' and describes it as being 'fully immersed in a feeling of energised focus'. I think of HPS in football as armour that protects you from falling victim to environmental, social or emotional wounds. The game is yours and no one and nothing can stop you from taking it. As I've said, players have different ways of entering a HPS: they play specific music, shout, run on the spot and more to become 'pumped up' and 'up for it'.

Everyone is different and accesses their most productive states in a different way. For example, Zlatan Ibrahimovic has said, 'I need to be angry to play.' This is something I can relate to. As a player, anger was a powerful way for me to enter a high performing state and protect me from performance insecurity. I was never visibly angry on the pitch, my anger was passive like the wind in a turbine overpowering negative belief messages from my brain.

Knowing how to access a resourceful or high performing state is the foundation for good performance and a fruitful career; we all do this in unique ways that fit our character.

When I play I set myself up to be in a positive state of mind. I focus on every detail of what happens around me, and during the game the voice in my head is confident, willing the attacker to shoot so I can save the ball. This helps a lot and has me performing at a high level. When I'm not in the team or I don't play as well as I want, it does get to me. When I make a mistake or concede a goal, I refer back to the voice in my mind and begin to coach myself. The voice in my head has limited time to coach for when the next challenge comes which could be within seconds. Usually I say to myself, 'Come on, turn the page right now, you still have time to help the team and be the hero!'

During my time at Malaga, I recall a game we played against Real Betis. I made a mistake that led to us conceding a goal. It was a really bad moment and what made matters worse was that both teams were in the relegation zone at the time, this match was a case of life and death (in footballing terms). The voice in my head was non-stop, asking, 'Why me? Why now? Blah, blah, blah.' Thirty minutes later a testing situation arose and I saved the ball. The voice in my head changed its tone and became more positive, telling me that this was the way to help my team and that I was good enough to do it. When playing in a relegation battle and your team is losing, the plan changes and you become vulnerable as a team as you attack in search of a goal. This is even more so as a keeper. During the Betis game, the ball was coming into my box more frequently than if we were winning or drawing. In the last second of the game, I pulled off a save to secure our victory.

I use this story as an example. Don't waste your time thinking about the mistakes you have made in a game during the game. You have the evening, the following days and post-match analysis to do that and, if needs be, you can train to rectify an un-useful habit. The focus should be on a quick recovery. Get yourself in the frame of mind that can support your performance as quickly as you can, because the game will bring you a new opportunity to help your team and you need to get through it.

—**Willy Caballero**
Chelsea and Argentina international

Performance insecurity

As every year passes, players are giving more to the game: more time, more effort and more of their life. They are leaving their families and friends at a younger age, losing the bonds that others have the chance to create. Either they have literally moved away from home to a football family home (digs) or they have mentally 'moved away' because of the increased commitment required. Football is their life. I refer to this time as the 'slow spin' because it is like those final few moments in roulette when the wheel slows down. It's a very heightened time with extreme focus, especially if you have invested everything. Young players need clear channels of communication, and they need to feel their issues and concerns are being heard, but often this is not the case.

Communication within football is limited, and as a result players regularly get upset because they feel they have been lied to or that management have not taken time to speak to them. They have invested so much of their lives in football, yet the dream they longed for as a child can turn into a nightmare. They know their families are dependent on them and this leaves many players extremely vulnerable and stressed. It's little wonder that they are constantly pulling information from their environment and trying to make sense of it. One common example of this is performance insecurity. Something as simple as a manager selecting a team for a training game or shadow play can be a trigger for instant anxiety. Players become hypersensitive in these situations, assuming that this is going to be the line-up of the team in the next official match, and if they are not chosen for this practice game, they will not be playing for the official team either. It can cause an instant change in state. Sometimes it's not noticeable, at other times there will be a change in body language, lack of interaction and effort, or a dip in performance. Some crumble, some turn

aggressive and rebellious, becoming a destructive influence in every team they play in. They don't want to experience those moments of victimhood or rejection again and see aggression as a way of taking control. Their self-destructive hypersensitive state is not a result of present circumstances, but of a past situation.

The state of those in charge

One of the most fundamental ways for a coach or manager to help players out of unresourceful states is to help them develop an awareness of their own behaviour: how they come across to others. Players will find it hard to control their own emotional state if they don't have a positive relationship with the person that leads them. That staff member may even be causing their unresourceful state, in which case they need to take steps to put this right.

Your manager is your friend. But he's not your best friend.
—**Christian Benteke**
Crystal Palace and Belgium international

Here are some questions coaching staff can ask themselves to assess how sensitive they are to this issue. Players can also ask themselves these questions (using the wording in brackets) to gain clarity about how they feel about their coach:

- Are you approachable? (Are they approachable?)
- Do you spread praise among the group? (Do they spread praise among the group?)
- Do you spread criticism? (Do they spread criticism?)
- Do you tailor delivery of criticism to the person you're giving it to? (Do they tailor delivery of criticism to the person they are giving it to?)
- Do you listen? (Do they listen?)
- Do you have a relationship with your players? (Do they have a relationship with the players?)
- Are you always coaching, or do you sometimes take the position of the learner? (Are they always coaching, or do they sometimes take the position of the learner?)
- Do you emotionally share yourself? Can you relate your personal experiences to what your players are going

though? (Do they emotionally share themselves? Can they relate their personal experiences to what their players are going though?)

These are simple questions, but the answers can be extremely useful and eye-opening.

The mental part of the game has become more of a topic of discussion due to pressure from social media, sponsors and owners, who are much more hands on. Pressure is part of the game, so the psychological aspect of football is something the player must develop in order to improve their chances of success.

I believe how you think affects your performance. If you're positive, you'll have a positive performance. If you're thinking negatively, you'll have a negative performance. I always think positively about future playing situations to give myself a positive feeling going into the game. When I feel bad about my performances, I turn to my family or my personal mental coach. I have moved to Italy to play for Lazio and now England to play for Southampton FC and I feel as though I have developed as a player and as a person. I feel capable of managing the extra things that come with the football environment.

—**Wesley Hoedt**
Southampton and Holland international

Awareness of state

It is easy to get lost in unresourceful states, unless you're Jose Mourinho. I often focus on football's behavioural blind spots and during the 2010 Champions League campaign, Mourinho pulled off a moment of brilliance that was missed by most.

Mourinho's Inter Milan were facing Pep Guardiola's Barcelona at Camp Nou. The score was 1-3 to Inter Milan on aggregate going into the game, Inter Milan's Thiago Motta was sent off with more than an hour to play against a team that was regarded as one of the best teams ever. Mourinho later said that at the time of the sending off, Barcelona were celebrating like their job was done. He walked over to the Barcelona technical area while Pep Guardiola was giving Zlatan Ibrahimovic instructions and whispered in Guardiola's ear, 'You think it's over, but it's far from over.'

In an ITV documentary about Mourinho, he explained the reason behind his comment was to motivate himself. We've looked at examples of players carrying out rituals to enter high performing states, but a manager performing to get a boost too? Who does that? What Mourinho did that day demonstrated his awareness of state and how to change it. It also shows that Mourinho truly sees himself as part of the team and his players do too.

Winning self mentality

Whether in everyday life or on the football field, most of us have never been taught about our state and how to manage it. We react without thinking, our responses based on experiences or what's happening around us. It just doesn't occur to us that we can take responsibility for how we feel and start operating in the most productive way possible. Yet the ability to identify your own state – maintaining it if it's effective, changing it if it isn't – is a vital skill to master. We've seen how Claudio Ranieri changed his team's collective state with a joke, how Jose Mourinho was aware of his own state and changed it from negative to positive at the Camp Nou and we will see later how state affects everything: your thinking, decision-making, communication skills, emotions, health and functionality. We all have the tools to enable us to choose our state and establish control over it.

In football this means your physical performance is less likely to be negatively affected by your state. There are many ways to develop an awareness of state, learn how to change state, and maintain an effective state. Sports psychologists or coaching staff are there to help, but emotional illiteracy is high among players. They just can't see how their performance is being held back or potentially how far it could go, so many of them don't take up that option. The performance specialists themselves have to be skilled in creating a high level of engagement with the players they are teaching otherwise they risk not getting through to them or creating even bigger emotional barriers. State must be explained lightly to give a clear understanding.

I feel one of the most effective methods of state training in football is through group personal development classes, otherwise known as my 'Winning Self Mentality' programme. In this programme, players take part in a mix of serious, fun, engaging and challenging talks and activities where they learn about different types of states and their meanings. They discover the triggers hidden in their blind spots and learn how to maximise their performance and improve their wellbeing through the management of state. It can be difficult to get an individual player to buy into something he feels he doesn't need, but a group discussion using his story as an example, or a situation where he passively learns from somebody else, can create a breakthrough. That's why group work is so important.

When approaching psycho-emotional topics, both the player and the performance specialist must be prepared to work with current problems and those which have their roots in the past. A player's current unresourceful state may be linked to many years of their parent telling them they'll never amount to anything in life, for example, and this can be challenging to eradicate.

For those who are not at a professional club and who don't have the option of a professional advisor, I would suggest creating your very own Winning Self Mentality sessions after training with your team:

1. **Feelings:** Pick a feeling to discuss, for example happiness, anxiety, excitement, panic or fear.
2. **Models of excellence:** Ask players to discuss examples of that feeling shown by professional players and what effect it had on their performance.
3. **Bringing the feeling into the room:** Players share a time when they experienced the same incident as the professional player or had the same feelings. They also talk about a time when they think a teammate in the room experienced that feeling too. It's a good idea to use the last match as a reference as it's fresh in their minds. Tip: All conversations must be about feelings and must be owned by the person saying them. Listen out for comments like 'they say' or 'people usually' and redirect them to say 'I think', 'I feel' or 'I do'.
4. **Reflect:** Ask the group if the conversation has brought anything up for them, maybe helping to explain why they felt or performed a certain way during a particular match. Do they see a closer connection now between feelings and performance?

If you're a parent you can use this conversation with your children, but only if they have already established some degree of emotional opening-up around football beforehand and have an awareness of state themselves. Because the performing state might be linked to childhood situations off the field, it's important for the parents of young players to be 'state aware' so they can improve the support they provide, both inside and outside the football environment.

Family is key in the development of the player. Two of the young Dutch internationals I interviewed for this book, Wesley Hoedt of Southampton FC and Bart Ramselaar of PSV Eindhoven, emphasised how important the emotional support of their family had been to their development as footballers.

The coach gets the best out of me when I really feel his belief and faith in me, whether I play well or not. If I feel that I have his support, I will feel comfortable to play without worry, without doubt and without me feeling anxious about what he is thinking. Once he gives me that solid foundation to build my performance on, I will feel empowered to attack the day!

—**Besard Sabovic**
Djurgardens IF and Sweden Youth international

Professor Jocelyn Faubert is a highly respected Canadian psychophysicist who has conducted extensive research on how the construction of internal images is fundamental to a player's performance. His NeuroTracker program trains a player's cognitive abilities and includes a system where players create an internal image of a situation and then make an effective decision. It enables elite players to reach the next level of performance by helping them envision situations of extreme emotional intensity, for example taking a penalty during a World Cup final. Obviously, this is something you can't practise in real life, even if you take penalties all day long! Scoring a penalty in training is followed by going inside for a shower; scoring in the World Cup final will potentially create history, and that affects how you think, feel and kick!

I discussed state management with Professor Faubert and he agreed that if the player is not emotionally sound, his system doesn't work. This is why state management is so crucial and can override everything – tactics on the day, training throughout the week and even a lifetime commitment to the game. Master your state and you will always be operating from a place of resourcefulness and emotional balance.

> In the next chapter, we will examine the importance of the mind–body connection, using unconscious competence as an example. To be so comfortable that you find yourself 'in the zone' more and more often.

TWO

UNCONSCIOUS COMPETENCE

In our craft, habit makes you the best

—Colin Kazim-Richards
Corinthians and Turkey international

The mind–body connection plays a huge role in performance of any kind, particularly sport. The dream scenario is to be able to perform consistently at an optimum level without consciously thinking about the nuts and bolts of what you're doing. You are 'in the zone', reacting instinctively and successfully, because your body and mind are in perfect harmony. Everybody has experienced that feeling, even though it may not have been while playing sport. Psychologists call it 'unconscious competence'.

I define unconscious competence as the ability to do something successfully or efficiently without consciously focusing on it. Zlatan Ibrahimovic describes it well in his book *I am Zlatan Ibrahimovic* when he says, 'It was like a dance, and even though I wasn't conscious of it, I dribbled past every one of the defenders … and toed the ball into the net with my left foot.' He goes on to describe how, when he was a junior, he practised 'for hours and hours until I could do it in my sleep and didn't even need to think in order to pull it out of the bag. It just came naturally.'

The four stages of competence

When we learn something new, we go through different stages taking us from zero beginner to expert. Ibrahimovic was talking about reaching the final stage, but not all of us will reach a level of unconscious competence for every skill. Here are the stages:

Level 1 – *Unconscious incompetence*
When you do something for the first time, you know very little about it and you can't do it. You want to improve but there's a problem: you don't know what you don't know. To move up to the next level you must acknowledge the level you are at and the value of the new skill.

Example: In the summer of 1997, when I was 14 years old, I watched Brazil play France in the opening game of the Le Tournoi tournament. Brazil were awarded a free kick 35 yards from the French goal. Roberto Carlos stepped up to take the free kick for Brazil and smashed the ball with the outside of his left foot. The ball looked like it was heading away from the goal, only to change direction and slam into the back of the net. Every football lover in the world was talking about the goal and it blew my mind. I wanted to copy not so much the goal but the technique, but I didn't know how.

Level 2 – *Conscious incompetence*
You are aware of what you don't know and the value of the new skill in addressing the shortfall. Mistakes are very important at this stage because each mistake provides more understanding and feedback.

Example: I went to my school, Sedgehill, hopped over the fence to the playing field and began to practise the free kick. I had little success at first but made mental notes of each failure. I went back to the video I'd recorded of the goal and watched it again and again. I also listened to interviews from Roberto Carlos, trying to get tips on how to improve the technique.

Level 3 – Conscious competence
You are good at doing something but it's not automatic, it still needs your attention and mental energy. Conscious competence requires all your conscious focus.

Example: After I felt that I had collated enough information on how to replicate the free kick, I spent numerous hours a week practising. Standing 15 yards in front of the goal and in line with the post, I swiped my left foot across the ball and watched it curl outwards, then curl inwards. I could do it! But only occasionally and only if I concentrated.

Level 4 – Unconscious competence
This is the move from doing something with full attention to doing it automatically. The way to get from conscious competence to unconscious competence is through practise, continuous repetition.

Example: After hours and hours of practise, I could confidently use the outside of my foot with only a fraction of the effort and concentration I'd used on Sedgehill's playing field. I was comfortably shooting and passing short and long. That was the time in my footballing career when I used the outside of my boot more often, and with a higher level of technical ability, than I had ever done before.

David Beckham is hard working. I used to watch him after training. You know his signature Bend it Like Beckham free kicks? He was able to do them because, after training, he would repeatedly practise. It wasn't a case of him just taking the free kicks; he would get the balls after training and practise – boom, boom – again – boom, boom – improving his technique.

Cristiano Ronaldo used to repeatedly practise his step-overs. He put the ankle weights on – vroom, vroom, vroom, vroom – ankle weights off – vroom, vroom, vroom, vroom. His feet were like windscreen wipers.

—Quinton Fortune
former Manchester United and South Africa international

Once you reach the level of unconscious competence, the problem is accessing it all the time. So many things can affect performance, like your emotional state, your physical fitness, your beliefs and confidence. In one match you may be able to play effortlessly and without thinking; in the next you may find you are struggling like a novice. It's something professional sports people have to deal with all the time and why sports psychologists have jobs. One former pro footballer told me about his experience of just that issue:

I played for England at youth level alongside my strike partner Michael Owen and went on to score goals in the Premier League. I'm one of only five people to score a hat-trick against Liverpool. But I didn't feel I really belonged until I was 29.

Before that, I would play in the first team and do what I felt was required of me, but I wasn't scoring like I did in the reserves. Because I was a first team player coming down to the reserves, it felt as though I was helping them out, so I was able to just play, like I was on autopilot.

Ironically, a time I was able to do this in the first team was the week after I got booed by my own fans. Why? 'Cos I didn't give a shit. I stopped caring, I stopped thinking and just played. Everything I did came off. And that was also the week I scored the hat-trick against Liverpool.

—Kevin Lisbie
former Charlton and Jamaica international

Kevin had reached such a high level of skill that he could play without thinking, but he couldn't do it all the time. It wasn't a problem of physical fitness, but mental attitude. His mind, his beliefs and his emotions affected his performance. The mind is key, so let's look at its role in unconscious competence.

How your mind manages you

The brain is the most important and powerful tool we have as humans, and it plays a crucial role in the performance of footballers.

It's where the game is won and lost.

—Luis Da Silva
Stoke City and Portugal international

Scientists disagree about the exact figure, but the consensus is that our unconscious mind manages around 80 to 95 per cent of our thoughts and our conscious mind manages the other five to 20 per cent. Maybe you think that's surprisingly low, but there's a reason for it.

We're bombarded by a massive amount of information every day. We process between two and 11 million bits of information per second including imagery, sound, touch, smells, temperature and taste. We can only focus consciously on 50–134 bits per second or our brains would explode. (Well, maybe not actually explode, but you know what I mean!) So, we filter out by deleting, distorting and generalising most of it and focus on the bits which we feel are relevant to us.

The part of you that is noticing things and focusing on them, both in your head and in the world outside, is your conscious mind. It allows you to have a subjective experience and to choose to behave in a way that you think best fits the situation. It pays attention when you are doing something unfamiliar, new or important to you, like having to follow a diversion on the way to work or thinking of how to respond to a difficult text from a friend, but otherwise is on automatic pilot. West Ham United's centre midfielder Mark Noble had just this experience.

The 2015/2016 season was West Ham United's last at the Boleyn Ground before their move to the Olympic Stadium. For their first game of the 2016/2017 season Mark found he had driven to the Boleyn Ground without consciously thinking. He then realised his mistake and turned the car round. He later described his journey as being on autopilot.

That autopilot was Mark Noble's unconscious mind, which handled the complex task of driving a vehicle and navigating safely from A to B without him even being consciously aware of it. If you drive, I'm sure you'll have had this experience too.

The unconscious mind

Like a computer running programs in the background, your unconscious handles everything from digesting food and transporting oxygenated blood around the body, to routine tasks like driving to work along a familiar route. Some programs run by the unconscious mind are put there when we were younger. Lots of reactions, habits or phobias are connected to long-forgotten incidents that happened years before. Sometimes therapy and significant moments can uncover these.

Things can move from the conscious mind to the unconscious as they become more familiar and you stop noticing them. This also works the other way around and something out of place can jolt things back from your unconscious to your conscious mind. For example, if you know a friend's living room really well, you don't pay attention to it when you visit them. Then one day you go in there and think, *hmm, something's not right.* You say, 'What have you done? Have you moved something? Been redecorating?' Your friend's-living-room-always-looks-like-this program has been interrupted, so you notice it. Once you get used to the new scheme, it will move back again.

How does this apply to football? You may have heard footballing staff yell 'instinct', or 'habits' or 'decision-making' across the pitch during training. What they're referring to is unconscious competence. Footballers rely on it; they're judged on it all the time, but it's never really discussed in great depth even though it's so crucial. And just like Mark Noble using complex skills – navigation, driving ability, spatial awareness – to get him to the Boleyn Ground on autopilot, he will also be using complex skills on the pitch, as does any pro footballer.

Three seconds

Ronaldo Luis Nazário de Lima was the best; he did the most difficult things so easily. Roberto Baggio was my second favourite. He was a champion of humility; Roberto knew he was a super talent but he was always trying to help others. His technique was superior but what I admired most was his ability to see things on the field in advance.

—**Raffaele Buondonno**
former Inter Milan striker

Unconscious competence is a big deal. Look at what a player has to do from the second before they receive the ball to the second after they have possession, a total of three seconds. In that time, they need to:

1. Visualise the different options open to them once they get the ball, so that they can select and apply an action within milliseconds.

2. Decide how to receive the ball.
3. Decide what to do with their first touch.
4. Be aware of space.
5. Be aware of their teammates.
6. Be aware of their opponents.
7. Assess the capability of their opponents.
8. Select the weakest person to face in that scenario.
9. Choose whether to dribble, pass or shoot.
10. Be aware of the different parts of their body.
11. Coordinate the parts of their body.
12. Be aware of the ball.
13. Be aware of what will happen after they give the ball to a teammate.
14. Think of the appropriate technique to use and how the ball will arrive to the teammate.
15. Select the technique.
16. Think of which foot to use.
17. Assess whether ball is in the right place to connect effectively.
18. Execute.

Incredible, isn't it? In three seconds they have to process 18 things. (In fact, once they receive the ball, they have 14 things to think about in a split second.) And remember, this is in a situation where things change every half a second! This is not something that is being handled by the player's conscious mind.

Cognitive psychologist George A. Miller says, 'The number of objects an average human can hold in working memory is seven, plus or minus two.' That means we can consciously focus on between five and nine things at a time. So, 18 things in the space of three seconds, which I'll refer to from now on as the 3–18, are being processed unconsciously. Top level football is extremely fast both physically and mentally. It relies heavily on the ability to act without consciously thinking as players are continually constructing internal scenarios and executing them. The best players we have ever seen have done great things physically, but it's the thought behind what they do that makes them work. Cristiano Ronaldo is reported to run at speeds ranging from 20.3 to 24.4 miles per hour. Most people only manage to go that fast when they're in a car and can still have an accident if they don't manage to make the correct decision in time. Ronaldo is a great player, and he will go down in history for many reasons. His attributes are often broken down into two elements: his skill and his hard work, but I would add another to the mix. You cannot be that great without having strong unconscious competence. To travel at those speeds and have to process the unconscious 3–18 continuously is a challenging task, one which forms the foundation of Ronaldo's success.

When things go wrong

In our 3–18, point ten is be aware of the different parts of their body. I want to explore this a bit more, because it's something we all take for granted, even though it's absolutely crucial.

Our body is constantly communicating, that's its job. It does this in multiple ways, including sending messages to other people through body language or running a dialogue between the brain and other parts of the body. And we navigate harmoniously through life and football, until injury or illness strikes.

When there's a breakdown in communication you know about it; the smallest tasks turn into huge chores. You know when you're at the dentist and they've numbed your mouth? It's a really weird feeling, because your tongue is being sent messages from the brain, but no messages are being sent back. This strange experience makes you conscious of what is going on in your mouth; you might even need to focus on how to form words, something you don't even think about in everyday life.

Imagine that dentist experience throughout most of your body. This is exactly what happened to Ian Waterman, subject of the BBC documentary *The Man Who Lost His Body*. At 19, Ian got a virus that was deemed incurable and he was advised to use a wheelchair. The virus destroyed half his nervous system and his 'position sense'. Because parts of his body were not communicating back to his brain, Ian had to look at his limbs to see what their position was and if they were moving or not.

Determined to lead as normal a life as he could, Ian began to develop new neural pathways. Now, every day, like a puppet master, he has to make his body work in the way he wants it to. He does this by directing it with his mind, using his eyes as guides. He says, 'If I look away from my hand I lose all connection with it.' If Ian was sitting down holding a cup in a room at night and someone switched the light off so he could no longer see his hand, he would drop the cup. The same would happen if he were to stand in a room and the light was switched off, he would fall.

This happens when a baby stands for the first time. You can see the focus on their face as they try to master the mammoth task of standing on two legs. Once they manage it, all the adults in the room clap and cheer, the baby's attention shifts from self-management to looking and laughing at the audience and – crash! (Thank God for the padding of nappies.) Babies have to consciously learn actions before handing the task over to their unconscious.

Ian can't do that though. He finds tasks like walking mentally draining because every movement requires conscious thought. If he is distracted for a second, he loses the understanding of where his left and right foot are in relation to each other and where he has placed his balance. In the documentary, we learnt that when a pretty lady stole his attention for a moment, Ian lost his balance for the first time in a while because he stopped thinking about the management of his legs and started thinking about what he would like to do if he was with her.

Proprioception

The problem Ian has is that he has no 'position sense' in much of his body. The technical term for this position sense is proprioception and it's a fundamental aspect of unconscious competence in sport.

Proprioception is the unconscious perception of movement and spatial orientation needed to maintain balance. It results from information detected by nerves and passed onto the brain via the eyes and the semi-circular canals of the inner ear. Neurologist and physician Oliver Sacks calls it 'an unconscious sense that allows us to move normally'. This probably sounds much too complex for the football pitch, but the more you refine your proprioception skills, the richer, more natural and easier your movements become.

I know quite a bit about proprioception because of my personal experience of injury.

Making the connection

'What I want you to do is put your weight on one leg and dribble the ball around it with the other leg.' I looked at the physio, David Wales, known as Walesy, as if he had lost the plot. I was in serious pain, and had been out of the game for six weeks with a medial ligament injury. That morning I'd already done 24 minutes on the treadmill at three-quarter pace, 24 minutes on the bike at three-quarter pace, three sets of ten on the leg curl and three sets of ten on the leg extension, along with a sprinkle of bench presses for my ego. I was in no mood for anything else weird and wonderful, so I opened my mouth to protest, but Walesy was having none of it. 'You need to do some proprioception work,' he said. 'End of.'

Walesy was the best physio at Charlton Athletic at the time and went on to work at Arsenal. Had it been anyone else I would have told him where to get off. I was 17 at the time and quite opinionated, but this was a guy I trusted implicitly. Still, I wasn't quite sure what he was on about this time. 'Proprio what?'

'Proprioception. Position sense. You've basically damaged the connection between your brain and your knee.'

'So, you're saying this'll help improve my balance?'

'No Kevin, this'll help you relearn *how* to balance.'

Back then, I played football mostly in my head and not my body. Instead of trusting my abilities and immersing myself in the experience, the flow if you like, I was always questioning my decisions and my capabilities. Ironically, this injury had happened during one of the few times I was completely absorbed, almost in a kind of daydream. I was playing for Charlton Athletic Under-17s in the Youth Premier League against West Ham at home at the Sparrows Lane training ground. Playing against West Ham was always a big thing for me, not because it was a London derby, but because I was playing against my old club and former teammates.

I don't remember the score that day, but I do remember that in the second half the game began to open up. I'd just broken up a West Ham attack on the edge of our area and I began to gallop towards the halfway line. Travelling with the ball was a strength of mine and this was one of those rare occasions when I was in the zone; my mind faded into the background as my body took over. It seemed to me like all the players and observers had fallen completely silent.

Everything around me moved in slow motion. Then... BANG! Like a fast train into central London, West Ham's Glen Johnson wrapped two reality checks around my left leg.

I snapped back into my head, the sounds around me returned, things began moving at normal speed and I realised that I was rolling around on the floor just past the halfway line, hoping the friction would dull the worst pain I had felt in my life. My left knee was swelling up like a bowling ball.

As the physio helped me to the side of the pitch, I could hear the dialogue from some of the players from both sides, including Glen's voice saying the tackle wasn't that bad. My manager at the time Mick Browne began giving me grief about taking too many touches – in his world more than two touches was too many. I was already fuming and his comments made me even angrier. I was furious with myself for not noticing someone lunging at me from the front and upset that a friend had tackled me like that. In an instant, I had gone from being almost in a trance, trusting my body and with my mind on autopilot to a situation where I was letting my emotions run riot. Even back then, I knew that wasn't a good thing.

Now, Walesy was telling me that a part of my body had become like a stranger. It made me feel uncomfortable. I didn't want to be baby Kev, having to consciously learn to balance again. I wanted my left knee to reintegrate with the rest of me.

After a short while, I began to enjoy the proprioception exercises. They were the easiest parts of my very intense rehab because they usually involved ball skills. As far as I was concerned, the more proprioception I could do, the quicker I could get out onto the field with my teammates.

Walesy talking about the connection between my mind and my body really made an impression on me. Up until then, everything I'd done in football and during my rehab was about physical functionality. The injury and the rehab made me realise that I depended on skills that I was not aware of to play football.

Between two minds
The unconscious mind can do wonders for your performance, but it's not good to play the whole game unconsciously, nor is it very likely you could. Some of the greatest play sequences and victories from individual players and teams have been as a result of quite conscious, calculated moves and decisions on the pitch, not split-second reactions.

During the 2000 FA Youth Cup with West Ham United at Upton Park, I had to man-mark Joe Cole. I kept so close to him during that game that I knew the rhythm of his heart beat. From the first whistle, I felt his discomfort and annoyance, but after 30 minutes he began playing strategically. Joe sacrificed his time with the ball to pull me all over the pitch. He realised that I was going to follow my instructions to keep tabs on him every step of the way. So, although we were up against each other in centre midfield, he took me into the wings and defences of both teams because it created a huge gap in the middle of the pitch for Leon Britton to exploit and Jermain Defoe to drop into. The result was 4 – 1 to West Ham, job done.

To be clever consciously and unconsciously and be able to move between the two is key. Some players unconsciously float into the right places at the right time to receive the ball. Others see the game almost geometrically, analysing space in real time or collating data from the first part of the game (like Joe did) and coming up with a strategy.

These problem-solving strategies come from the conscious mind. Those who play purely on instinct using the unconscious mind will be able to take part in the game but not take control of it. There have been many super talented players who have struggled to get into a Sunday league team or a Premier League team because they can't 'think on their feet'.

Although this chapter is about unconscious competence, we must never underrate the importance of conscious competence. I have chosen not to go into great depth about the conscious mind because it's something that's discussed by football pundits all the time in the media and in pubs, offices and homes up and down the country. The involvement of the unconscious, on the other hand, barely gets a look-in.

Training for unconscious competence

An understanding of unconscious competence is of vital importance in football. To reach your full potential you must continuously monitor your own performance with the understanding that hard work now pays dividends later. When you're training, always remember there's a long-term objective. You're not just doing it for its own sake; you're not wasting your time. That long-term objective is to combine physical and mental training in order to reach a level of unconscious competence in a number of key skills. To have practised something so much that it becomes automatic. Five-a-side football is a good example of combining a hard mental and physical workout, particularly for defenders. There are attackers closer to their goal than the defenders would like and this feeling of vulnerability heightens the senses. To add to this vulnerability, they constantly have to decide which strategy to use to stop the opposition scoring.

Goalkeeper training is another good example of conditioning the unconscious. Keepers save a shot from one angle, are given one second to recover, then have to save a shot from another angle. Using the same method, the training can become more complex with keepers having to claim crosses between shots or carry out movement sequences (quick feet), all with the aim of occupying the mind and giving it a challenge that it must respond to in a fraction of a second.

Goalkeeper coaches use a lot of creative exercises from other sports. When the other keepers and myself train, it's important that we know why we are doing the training and it's important that we enjoy the training. For example, we do ping-pong speed competitions (where machines serve balls at you fast); this exercise is to develop our reactions. We then extend the level of difficulty by adding cognitive elements to increase our ability to think quicker in different situations.

—Willy Caballero,
Chelsea and Argentina international

Some football coaches are aware of the importance of developing the unconscious mind. Belgian coach Michel Bruyninckx has developed a brain-centred method for footballers, known as CogiTraining. He has coached at Anderlecht, Standard de Liège, Belgian FA and Aspire Academy, and he has been credited for playing a key role in the emergence of the Belgium national team. Players such as Napoli FC's Dries Mertens and FC Porto's Steven Defour were under Bruyninckx's tutelage. I had the pleasure of meeting him when he came to London in May 2011 to speak at Bacon's College School Sports Partnership Coaching Conference. This gave me the opportunity to hear about his strategies at first-hand. I was very impressed to learn that apart from the improvement in their football, Bruyninckx's brain training methods resulted in participants improving their school results by an average of ten per cent.

Bruyninckx's method trains players to perform sequences without any psychological rest time. Repeatedly carrying out twists and sharp turns, and with sequences that require the whole team, players have to judge the weight of their pass and assess the right time to navigate into space.

At the introduction to a session, players form four small queues on the four points of a compass-shaped grid. The people at the front of the four queues run into the middle, perform an action given by Bruynnickx prior to the start of the session and then leave. Players may be told, for example to dribble into the middle, stop the ball, run across the grid, take the ball from the person in front of you, do a Cruyff Turn, dribble back and pass the ball to the next person in the line.

Once the team are comfortable with this, the session develops in complexity, with everyone moving at the same time performing different actions. The players get used to being in a busy environment, carrying out positive habits over 500,000 times per season. As Bruyinckx puts it, 'If you do something 500,000 times, its less likely that you will have to consciously think about it.' I suggest you type 'VT176 – Michel Bruyninckx' into YouTube to watch progressive circuits that give clear examples.

Outside football, specific skills like proprioception can be enhanced and developed through doing Yoga, Wing Chun, T'ai Chi and Qi Qong with eyes closed because we are so dependent on the eyes to give moment-by-moment feedback on our balance. I've done Tai Chi, Qi Qong and Yoga for two years and have noticed great improvement in my flexibility, strength, mobility and mental health.

> Mastery of the senses is an essential element in the development of an all-rounded player, not just the physical senses of vision, hearing and touch but a sixth sense too – telepathy. That's what we are going to examine next.

THREE

MIND, BODY AND EYES

It's Tuesday, 26th September 2017, inside the Vodaphone Arena, home of Besiktas Football Club. Most of the 36,641-strong crowd sport the black and white colours of the home team, the simplicity of the strip contrasting with the vibrant energy level. It's Champions League time. Besiktas are playing RB Leipzig and the roar of the Besiktas fans is so deafening that RB Leipzig's German international forward Timo Werner begins to feel dizzy and opts to wear earplugs so he can carry on with the game. It's a risky decision because doing this means cutting off a major source of information. He isn't able to hear shouts of 'man on!', 'time!' or 'left shoulder!' (mark the player to your left), sounds that prevent you from conceding and help you to score. So how would Werner perform on one of the biggest stages in world football without access to this information?

Decision-making in football is seen as the god of skills. It's spoken about often, its importance is respected, and yet it isn't developed in a systematic way, it just kind of happens. In a game where the scene changes every 0.5 seconds, ideas must be communicated and executed almost immediately. Footballers are skilled in pulling information from their environment and communicating it to their teammates through words and body language.

During play, there's a two-movement formula, mainly adopted by strikers. They make one movement then make a second in the opposite direction. They're not looking for the ball in the first movement, the run is a decoy move to deceive the defending player, but it also indicates to their teammate that they want the ball played to them on the second movement. For example, a striker may come short for the ball, then spin and run behind the defence with the expectation of receiving the ball as they move beyond the defence, and vice versa. The two-movement formula is taught in youth football but not all players use it. This is when knowing your teammate is essential because you learn how often they use the two-movement formula and how it fits in with their other preferences. Eventually, you may know your teammate's style so well it can seem your understanding of each other is almost telepathic.

Some players form such a bond, working from a place of feeling and using telepathy to play the game and gain an advantage over their opponent. Telepathy comes from the Greek word *tele* meaning 'distant' and *pathos* or *patheia* meaning 'feeling, perception or experience'. Telepathy is the transfer of information from one person to another without using known sensory channels.

Telepathy

During their time at Manchester United in the late 90s, Dwight Yorke and Andy Cole were unstoppable and played a huge role in Manchester United winning the treble, which included the Champions League. The duo scored 53 goals in their first season and 46 goals the following season, producing such moments of magic that their relationship was referred to as 'eerie telepathy'. Individually, Yorke and Cole were top strikers. Together, they were something else. Each would help the other get possession, act as decoys, and create moves and sequences to open up goal scoring opportunities for the other. It's not often that clubs buy two strikers that have played together before, but when Yorke and Cole moved on from Manchester United, Blackburn Rovers decided to capitalise on the powers of the Telepathic Two by signing both of them.

Makélelé was seen as a model of excellence in telepathy, not because of his connection with his teammates, but because of his connection with the opposing team. Makélelé had the ability to predict the thoughts of the opponents and break up their attacks, providing freedom for his midfield partners and protection for his defence. He was also brilliant at interpreting body language and could pre-empt his opponent's next moves by reading how their eyes revealed their intention or the way they pulled their leg back to strike the ball. Zinedine Zidane benefitted greatly from Makélelé's telepathic skills as they gave him freedom on the pitch. Makélelé performed so consistently to a high standard that the defensive midfield role was named The Makélelé Role.

Most football observers don't rate defence skills as highly as attacking ones, because many of the top defenders use something you can't see – their minds. By using a mix of analytical skills, anticipation and intuition a defender can move into the right area and thus prevent an attack. However, this won't get any acknowledgement from the amateur observer because the thought process the player used was not visible. A spectacular and highly visible slide tackle, on the other hand, will get a round of applause. It's hard to acknowledge that telepathy has been used to stifle an attack, especially when it's carried out so early that a tackle isn't needed.

Unfortunately, one of the people who did not rate Makélelé's telepathic skills was the Real Madrid President Florentino Perez. Perez said that the team would not miss Makélelé, his technique was average, he lacked the speed and skill to take the ball past opponents, he wasn't a header of the ball, he rarely passed the ball more than three metres and that upcoming younger players would soon cause Makélelé to be forgotten. The response from Zidane was 'why put another layer of gold paint on the Bentley when you are losing the entire engine.'

In his 1971 book *Silent Messages*, documenting his research into non-verbal communication, Albert Mehrabian revealed that 55 per cent of communication is through body language like facial expressions, hand signals and gestures. We are not taught how to do this growing up, we just learn by experience. Some people are good at communicating and reading intentions using body language and others not so good. This plays a key role in player performance, as understanding a teammate's intentions is so important.

Verbal communication is an important part of decision-making. It helps players receive the ball, alerts teammates of danger, creates awareness of where they are on the field of play and relays tactical information. But when there are 60,000 fans chanting, it's not always easy to hear what your teammates are saying unless they shout, which means your opponents know your intentions and your strategy is no longer secret.

To be efficient in football, players must be able to predict where, when and how their teammates and the opposition will move and pass. They have to react before something happens. Responding too late means that the opposing defenders will be able to get back into the correct position and you will concede a goal or your teammate will wander offside. Being able to make the most of the information at hand is a fundamental part of the game, but how is it done?

What your body tells your opponent

During a football match, players reveal how they are going to play the ball in a variety of non-verbal ways, from how they position their bodies to where they look. There's a saying, 'The eyes are the windows to the soul.' In football, I believe the eyes are the windows to someone's ideas. The eyes are very important when defending, as they give the biggest clues to the decision the player in possession will make.

Players are continuously grabbing information from the pitch in search of options. Once they find those options, they react in different ways. Some will tense up in order to take action immediately; others will pretend they haven't seen an option, only to take it up a couple of seconds later. Pretending to take an opportunity and turn down the original one reduces the chance of losing possession because the new option you discovered has grabbed the defender's attention.

Former Manchester United and England midfielder Paul Scholes' head would consistently swivel during matches, his eyes collecting data at every turn. He used this information from the pitch, plus his instincts, to direct the performance of one of Britain's most successful teams ever.

Spain international and Chelsea midfielder Cesc Fabregas has a great eye for finding pockets of space on the football pitch, using information to stay away from his opponent, creating geometrical angles of space to receive the ball and cause danger, like playing a game of snooker.

Castrol Edge made a documentary on key elements of Cristiano Ronaldo's game, called *Tested to the Limit*. The documentary is regarded as using the most rigorous testing ever to have ever been carried out on a footballer. Two tests focused on Ronaldo's vision. The first was a one-on-one exercise where he had a ball and had to beat his makeshift defender, football consultant Andy Ansah. Ronaldo was equipped with eye trackers, which used a red dot to show where he was looking as he tried to beat his opponent. Ronaldo scanned places beyond the defender, taking the occasional look at the ball and the defender's knee and hip to see what information he could pull from him to predict his next move. Once he knew what the defender would do, he could then counter it. In eight seconds, Ronaldo executed 13 moves, including step-overs and drag backs, moves that were produced at great physical and mental speed.

The tests, in a lighted studio, were also carried out with an amateur player called Ronald, who was the same age and roughly the same height as Ronaldo. In the second test, Andy crossed a ball into the box for the player to finish, but a second after the ball left his foot the lights were switched off, so the player could make his move based only on Andy's body posture and the early flight of the ball. Ronald went first, trying to score from a cross that he had seen for one second once it left Andy's boot. The lights clicked off, the night vision camera clicked on. All Ronald could see was darkness. The night vision camera showed him guesstimating where he could meet the ball and missing by some distance. Then up stepped Ronaldo. Andy crossed. The lights went off. Bang! The camera crew started clapping as soon as they heard him make connection with the ball. The lights went back on, the ball was in the net and the night vision camera confirmed that he had scored. To make sure it wasn't luck, Ronaldo did it again, the second cross made more difficult because the bounce was just before him, but he executed a half volley. The narrator said that a human's reaction time is 200 milliseconds and by 500 milliseconds Ronaldo's unconscious had already interpreted Andy's body language, worked out the direction of the ball, calculated the speed and trajectory, and programmed his body to carry out the correct movements to meet the ball at the right moment. Ronald was unsuccessful because he was watching the ball instead of picking up information from Andy's body language so when the lights went out he had no information to guide him on where to go.

In the third part of the test, the lights were switched off as soon as Andy touched the ball, so Ronaldo only had Andy's body language to work from. Ronaldo did a cool finish into the bottom corner using the top part of his chest and part of his shoulder. Ronaldo, by his own admission, said that he was going to head the ball but was scared that it might hit his face so opted to use his shoulder and chest area instead. When you think about the large margin for error there too, it shows how much confidence he had with the limited information provided. The tests illustrated Ronaldo's unconscious proficiency, his ability to recall situations in training and games where he had used similar skills and then to apply the same action. It also demonstrated how effective he was at getting the most out of the smallest piece of information, a skill we see often from the 'fox in the box' type of players, and something Ronaldo uses regularly to great effect.

Knowingly and unknowingly players have their own particular micro or macro patterns, such as Joe Cole poking the inside of his cheek with his tongue when dribbling to Robin Van Persie's bird-like pose with arms stretched out by his sides and elbows dipped as he changes direction. Moving their eyes, tongue or arms a certain way, or using some other trademark gesture, is more often than not part of a pattern a player uses to execute a pass, a dribble, create space or shoot.

Every player on the football pitch is required to defend throughout a match. Attacking players are now judged on their defending more than ever before, so if you want to get the edge over your opponent during a match, you need to learn your opponent's patterns at the beginning of the game, depending on how often they receive the ball. A footballer needs to know the opponent's strongest foot in order to force him onto the weaker foot. They need to know their opponent's physical attributes, so they can counter them.

If you can use body language skills (non-verbal cues), it makes defending easier, wins the psychological battle and takes your performance to the next level.

I still play five-a-side-football and unless a player gives me something more obvious to read, I pay close attention to the eyes. I watch their eyes flick across the pitch in search of a solution; I notice their reaction when they've found an option. Once I have mentally stored their reaction to finding a solution, I'll reassess the process once or twice more. If it's the same, I now have that player's pattern nailed. Once I know their pattern, I can dominate them.

The eyes have it

In the therapeutic world there's a sarcastic joke: If I can't see it, then it doesn't exist. It's funny because the reasons people come to therapy and what they expect to get out of therapy are invisible.

In life there's a huge reliance on being able to see things, but not much attention is paid to the things we use for this – our eyes. One afternoon my wife asked me when I last got my eyes tested and I responded with one of my usual cheeky jokes, 'Obviously not before our wedding!' After she gave me 'the look', I went on to tell her that I have never had my eyes tested as I can see perfectly fine. Once she got over the shock, she began to educate me about eye health and I realised how much I relied on my eyes and took them for granted. I immediately got my eyes tested.

Professor Gail Stephenson told *Manchester Evening News* that 80 per cent of the information we use to carry out an action comes from our vision. Professor Stephenson is the person who wrote to Sir Alex Ferguson when Manchester United's form took a mini slump in 1996, to tell him that their loss of form was down to the kit they wore and not what was underneath. It was a grey Umbro kit, a colour that isn't easy to see during such a fast-moving game. As a result of this, Ferguson asked Professor Stephenson to provide eye training sessions at Manchester United, sessions that Gary Neville didn't see the value in during his playing days, admitting that at the time he didn't listen to her.

Professor Stephenson believed that players could react to situations quicker and be more effective overall if they improved the way they use their eyes, the improvement being the quality and speed in which they process information.

After being out injured, players had to include eye training as part of their sessions. It wasn't until he was reflecting on his career after retirement that Neville acknowledged the benefits. He now believes that being match fit isn't only about running; it's about the cognitive elements too.

All players use their eyes for a number of reasons, however, when an attacker has the ball, the person defending will be using their eyes that little bit more. Both are assessing their surroundings, trying to get one up on each other, looking for the slightest clue about their opponent's intentions.

For me, the game is about dominating your individual battles on the pitch. In my case, as a defender, it's my duty to dominate the striker. I feel that the start of the battle sets the tone, so I set out to give him a tough time and cause plenty of danger and not the other way around.

I want to intimidate the strikers I play against, so I try to look as big and hard as possible and show no weaknesses. Even when I'm tired I don't show it. How they see me is important and it's equally important that I play a role that gives me an advantage. I am always communicating with my teammates from my position on the pitch, and I purposely give arm signals to make my instructions crystal clear and to show my opponents I'm alert.

As a striker runs towards me with the ball, the body part I take the most information from is the face. I can't say specifically what I'm

looking for, but I assess every detail intensely for one to two seconds. That's enough time to give me an idea of what he's going to do. Then it's all about me, with my extra bit of information, against him. And that's my favourite part of defending.

—**Luca Ercolani**
Manchester United and Italy international

Every day people are playing football, whether it's a game between work colleagues or kids having a knockabout in the school playground. And when a player wins possession by using information the attacker has given unawares, you often hear them cheekily say, 'Read you like a book!'

What can an attacker do to prevent the defender from reading their intentions? Look away! Ronaldo proved that he could guess where the ball would go from assessing a player's body language alone, so to give your opponent more information is asking for trouble. Former Barcelona and Brazilian playmaker Ronaldinho became famous for his 'no-look' passes, throwing defenders off the scent and creating opportunities for his teammates. By looking away before passing, Ronaldinho was cutting off the information an opponent could use to anticipate his next move. The kind of information that former Real Madrid and France international Claude Makélelé thrived on when his opponents were attacking, information which helped him to protect his defence.

The eyes are the key to this information, so it's very important to train the eyes and use them skilfully. Players make errors on the pitch for many reasons, but a large number of mistakes are due to mismanagement of information or revealing too much information.

In discussing the eyes, I want to include 'the mind's eye'. Visualisation is popular among players and is done at any time from the evening before a match to the coach journey to the game. Pre-match visualisation helps to solidify responses. Players create internal movies of situations they might experience on the pitch, playing the scenes out in their minds and giving them successful endings so that if they were to encounter a similar scene in real life, they can access the stored response from their pre-match visualisation.

Everton and former England striker Wayne Rooney told

ESPN: 'Part of my preparation is I go and ask the kit man what colour we're wearing – if it's red top, white shorts, white socks or black socks. Then I lie in bed the night before the game and visualise myself scoring goals or doing well. You're trying to put yourself in that moment and trying to prepare yourself, to have a "memory" before the game. I don't know if you'd call it visualising or dreaming, but I've always done it, my whole life.'

Creating an internal movie involves the same thought patterns and stimulates the same muscles and electrical process that the brain uses during the actual activity. Therefore, imagining doing something improves your chances of executing it successfully during a match.

Elite skills

So much of football involves using the mind effectively, yet there isn't much training for players on how to process or manage the information they are exposed to. Some manage it naturally, some don't. That's why we have players with bundles of technical ability struggling with the psychological challenges of the game. Many don't perform to their full potential or they drop down the leagues and out of the game. Coaches have been baffled by this for years, unable to figure out what's been holding back their talented players.

If a player can't see clearly, or they struggle with information overload or they don't understand the value of the information they possess, they can misread angles and distances between teammates and rivals and end up giving too much information away. It takes great intelligence and application of psychology to be an effective player. The top performers in the game can access options that are almost invisible to the amateur eye all within a split second. This is one of the reasons behind many arguments on the football field with players longing to play with people 'on the level'. Wayne Rooney spoke to ESPN about his rapid development in comparison to his peers. 'You're a bit more advanced than the kids your age, so there are times on the pitch where you can see different things, but they can't obviously see it. So, then you get annoyed – they can't calculate.'

Top performers like Luca Ercolani see everything but only take in the fine details that will help win the overall battle. Top performers do not overload themselves with information. They have high levels of visual attention, the ability to select relevant information and filter out the irrelevant. Wayne Rooney operated at an elite level as a youngster and he operates at an elite level as a professional. He sees things that his peers can't. It might be a space for his teammate to exploit so he can feed them the ball in a more dangerous position. It might be that he wants to exploit the space himself but needs his teammate to see it and play the ball there, so he does not end up offside.

By their nature, professional footballers are in the elite, but then there are those who are the elite of the elite. Other players attribute almost superhuman skills to their astounding colleagues. As former Arsenal midfielder Paolo Vernazza said of Dennis Berkgamp, 'Dennis would see the unseeable in training.'

The motherboard of a footballer

Ronaldo demonstrated that situational awareness matters; Manchester United's 1996 team showed us that vision plays a key role; Luca Ercolani told me how he takes information from his attacker to get the advantage; Ronaldinho showed the world how he withheld information, and Wayne Rooney told of his frustration when playing with those who cannot process information at the same level he can. Every example shows that elite players are constantly asking themselves how they can improve the way they process information and make better decisions.

I spoke to neurophysics professor Jocelyn Faubert, who has run a series of tests on skills that scientists believe are fundamental to performance. After testing hundreds of elite senior players, elite amateur players and non-athlete university students, he noted that professional players scored higher on the tests. Referring to the complex processes that professional players carry out within their heads as 'gymnastics of the brain', Professor Faubert says footballers have unique intelligence. His co-creation of the 3D visual exercise NeuroTracker develops and rehabilitates the cognitive functions of elite players. The exercise uses eight spheres resembling tennis balls which bounce across the screen. Players are told to focus on four balls, and when the game stops they must identify the four they were initially told to focus on.

Coincidently, the morning after the interview I was working at Southampton FC's training ground and found out that they had invested in NeuroTracker, so I gave it a try. It tested a key skill expected of elite players – the ability to see the bigger picture while focusing on the smaller picture. I couldn't follow one ball because I had to track four, so I picked a spot on the screen to focus on and then exercised my ability to see movement outside my direct line of vision. Every success brought a tougher challenge as the balls speeded up and bounced off each other. The complexity of progressing through the levels highlighted my competitiveness and what a bad loser I am. In the end, after being overwhelmed with the information at hand, I quit because I knew I wasn't going to be able to turn my performance around before my taxi came! After I calmed down, I thought about how much the experience mirrored scenarios on the pitch, the standout example being when a defender focuses on the player in possession while acknowledging the runner outside their direct line of vision before activating the offside trap. Getting those types of decisions right is invaluable in football and that is why the service is used by the NHL, NBA and Premier League players. Manchester United invested $80,000 in NeuroTracker, and Atlanta Falcons quarterback and MVP winner Matt Ryan uses it as an integral part of his training, three times a week to be precise.

The whole idea behind NeuroTracker is to understand dynamic scenes and I was curious to understand how the brain does that. How does it process motion, how does it anticipate things and at a higher level how does it deal with complexity under pressure? When a lot of things are happening at once and you have to make a decision, you have to process all relevant information. So, I asked myself, what are the minimum requirements the brain needs to process complex dynamic scenes like football play, or even everyday activities such as driving or crossing the street? Once I started breaking down the cognitive elements involved, I realised there were some critical demands to perform effectively, such as dynamic attention, selective attention, working memory and the ability to manage distractors. I isolated those elements and generalised them using 3D multiple object tracking and created NeuroTracker.

A professional footballer has to have expertise. If you don't have expertise, you won't make accurate predictions of play or make the right decisions. With everything being equal, you'd expect that people who have the same level of experience and similar physical attributes, will have similar performance outcomes. However, what we see through NeuroTracker learning rates is that there is another performance dimension in the capacity of the brain to adapt to training. Top elite athletes seem to have a superior capacity to learn, improving at much faster rates than amateur athletes or non-athletes. They learn more and extract more about what they need to do than others. If you expose them to the same level of experience, they will get more out of it, their brain is more plastic (neuroplasticity), and this is a form of intelligence.

This notion attracted a lot of good media attention, and bad too, with some academics saying, 'Hey, I spent my whole life trying to get into medical school. How can you say these guys are smarter than me?' I didn't actually say they were smarter, but I do say brainpower is used for many different things, and elite sports performance requires special cognitive abilities in order to efficiently extract the right information, do it rapidly, select what's most useful, then process and execute optimal action-responses. It's a high-level brain capacity, intelligence is not just about things like solving differential equations, there are other ways to use the brain.

When dealing with complex, dynamic scenes, there's a specific mode or type of intelligence that you require, and that's what's needed to follow NeuroTracker targets. The mental resources involved are also plastic (neuroplasticity). The mental skills that the professional footballer needs to perform this kind of mental processing are fundamental. In effect they're the same skills my grandmother needs to cross the street, but at a different level and tempo, but she still has to process all these elements.

The question arises: how do you optimise NeuroTracker training effects over time? To that I ask, 'Would you put an inexperienced driver in downtown traffic?' The answer is no, because they have to get used to the pedals, the gear stick and how the whole process works. Once they can perform those skills to a good level you can then take them on the highway and go downtown; there's a progressive approach to achieving learning. This is the same with cognitive training in sports. When you're working with professional athletes, they're clearly already performing at a very high processing level. However, and somewhat surprisingly, they still have huge room for improvement in cognitive skills. Research has shown that the optimal way to utilise NeuroTracker is to firstly perform 15 sessions or more of just NeuroTracker in a sitting position. This isolates core training and consolidates rapid gains in a way that prepares the brain for learning. Then we introduce basic dual-task training, such as performing NeuroTracker while standing, or doing a balance exercise. Then more complex or sports specific tasks such as passing a football while NeuroTracking. The cumulative effect is that we extend the learning effects and achieve extremely high levels of combined mental and physical performance over time – which is ultimately what you need to perform at under pressure on the field. We have programmes where you use NeuroTracker for a week or a week and a half all day during pre-season like at Manchester United.

In one of our programmes we also add on decision-making tasks using motion captures of real football player movements, such as kicking, sliding and different types of passes. We then present these within the NeuroTracker environment, and the players have to maintain situational awareness while picking up the movement cues and use them to pre-empt whether the person will, say, kick to their left or to their right, while being aware of everything that is going on around them. We also have more specific tactical awareness programmes, which can involve recognising play scenes while under cognitive load.

Interestingly, there are also indications that this kind of cognitive training can play a part in player psychology and self-control. We have access to speed skaters that are the best in the world; one of the coaches had an interest in how his skaters managed their self-control. When they had a bad NeuroTracker performance he'd state, 'Your intelligence doesn't just fizzle, it's your emotions'. He'd then get them to do breathing exercises that brings them towards a resourceful state, and boom, their score goes up! That's when they realised their emotion is directly linked with their cognition. They're sharing mechanisms, sharing systems, the two go together and we can use one to leverage the other. But to use them together boosts performance even further.

—**Professor Jocelyn Faubert**
Psychophysicist at the University of Montreal
and co-creator of NeuroTracker

Mind and eye training

Visual skills and information management are important parts of the game. If you want to improve your eyes and cognitive function, then these may help you:

- **NeuroTracker:** 3D object tracking is used to develop the brain functions critical for learning, to help with processing information when performing and to make better decisions.
- **Ultimeyes:** Baseball team The Highlanders improved their visual acuity by 31 per cent. Players noticed an improvement in their sporting performance and in activities in their personal lives.
- **Axon Sports:** Develops cognition within sport. Their service is based on what you see, how you manage the information and how quickly can you respond to the information, making the correct the decision.

So, how did RB Leipzeg's Timo Werner function with his earplugs in during the Champions League game against Besiktas? Unfortunately, his circulatory problems became unbearable and led to him asking to be subbed off after 32 minutes!

> Understanding and processing information from the environment is a vital skill for players and underlines the role of the mind in football. The next thing we are going to look at is something that we all take for granted, is different everywhere, and has a strong influence, both good and bad, on the game. I'm talking about culture.

FOUR

CULTURE

The Oxford Dictionary defines culture as the ideas, customs and social behaviour of a particular people or society.

Culture can be passed down through the generations and demonstrated in many ways, for example through art, food, music or sport. A culture's values and beliefs shape the behaviour of its people, dictating what is considered right and wrong. It directs thoughts, words and actions, and the direction we grow, if growth happens at all.

Individual experiences on the journey through life play a key role in human performance, of course. But when individuals form a team, the group perform as one. This is where a country's culture or a company's culture can change how people behave within that space. This group has a collective psychological programming, a collective way of thinking, behaving and playing.

To take the example of a country's football teams, Italy are known for being defensively astute, Brazil are known for being skilful, Spain and Holland are known for being technical and England are known for passion. A country's culture outside football affects the culture inside football; culture changes the lens through which we view the game. During his playing days, former Barcelona and Spanish international Xavi Hernandez talked about the contrast between the football culture of England and Spain. He said that when former Liverpool and England international Jamie Carragher won the ball and booted it into the crowd he got a round of applause, whereas in Spain you would get nothing. It raises an interesting question: what conditions did Jamie Carragher meet to get a round of applause from English fans? Why would he have got nothing from the Spanish fans?

Conditions of worth

Airline company Korean Air suffered five crashes in an 18-month period during the late 90s. Author and researcher Malcolm Gladwell believes that thousands lost their lives not because of any fault with the planes, but because of the specific behaviour of people in the moment, behaviour he identifies as being part of South Korean airline culture.

Recordings of cockpit conversations just before the crashes happened were examined. The co-pilots could be heard identifying dangers ahead in an unassertive manner, making suggestions and, in some instances, offering different options. Gladwell points out that Korean pilots do not speak assertively to their superiors which was why, in his view, co-pilots in the cockpit at the time of the crashes either withheld information or delivered it submissively.

In support of Gladwell's view, a study of cultural psychology ranks South Korea second in the world for respect for authority, otherwise known as 'power distance'. Power distance has its pros and cons, but in the cockpit, the cons far outweigh the pros. The problem was improved by recruiting people who had different cultural behaviours, who re-educated those who took part in power distance and taught them English, a non-hierarchical language.

Power distance can also apply to football. In certain cultures, if players have too much respect for a person they consider their 'superior' it can affect the development and growth of the team.

So far, I have played in England, Greece, Turkey, France, Holland, Scotland and Brazil. Turkey's culture off the field holds back their performances on the field. In Turkey, people refer to those older than themselves as Abi, meaning big brother or elder. In Turkish football, the players refer to their main player or the guy who earns the most money as Buyuk, which means 'big Abi'. If he messes up on the pitch, his lower status, lower earning teammates will not challenge him.

Technically, Turkish players are unbelievably good but the power of the Abi holds back Turkish football. You only have to look at the Turks in Germany and Holland compared with those in Turkey. They're all Turkish, but the culture they grew up in was different and this is what allows their talent to show. The likes of Mesut Ozil, Emre Can and Cenk Tosun flourished in Europe and they are German Turks. Yes, the development from a physical aspect may be better in Germany and Holland, but in football the physical can only get you so far. We talk about leadership from the perspective of the manager and the player, and how important it is. Abi is about overpowering leadership and a misuse of power. Cultural politics holds Turkish football back. If you have a problem with the coach or don't play well, that's it. You have to train alone, and you might not get paid your wages. I remember having to train alone in random training spaces with limited facilities at random times. If I refused to go along with the punishment or questioned their rule, it would result in a heavy fine or my wages would be withheld.

—**Colin Kazim-Richards**
Corinthians and Turkey international

To understand the power and complexity of a culture we must understand the role that beliefs and values play. Beliefs and values are governed by conditions of worth, meaning conditions we think we must meet in order for people to value us. To return to the example above about the difference between playing in England and Spain, Jamie Carragher was brought up in a system where the defender was expected to win tackles and 'get rid of it!' ('it' being the ball). Defenders were singled out for praise if they did that, so naturally Carragher, and thousands more of his fellow defenders, adhered to the conditions and got the plaudits. In Spain, on the other hand, defenders were expected to win possession and immediately start an attack by passing the ball out. That's when they would get the applause.

Individuals pass these beliefs on to the up-and-coming generations via their family, schools, football clubs and media platforms using selectively chosen stories which play up the conditions of worth. That's why it's not uncommon to see pictures in the English press of English players shouting aggressively, whether after conceding a goal, scoring a goal, winning a match or losing a match. Passion is demonstrated by aggression. Showing that you have passion is a core condition in England and if a player or manager doesn't visibly demonstrate this, their commitment to the game is immediately questioned.

The repeated use of pictures of blood or words of war such as 'die for the club', shows where value is placed in English football. There are constant reminders of past heroes to prove the point. The famous Terry Butcher picture from the 1989 World Cup qualifier match showing his bloodied head has been used so often that Butcher himself said that there was more to his game than a bloodied shirt.

These subliminal messages lead to the concept of the fight being so deeply entrenched within the collective unconscious of organisations and individuals that it shapes the minds of young children who then become players, coaches, broadcasters, parents and fans. Any change to, or challenge of, this value is therefore met with caution and resistance. The fight becomes a condition of worth, the condition players feel they must meet in order to be praised and accepted by others. Parents and coaches filter the game they see and the feedback they give according to these conditions of worth and so the cycle continues.

A common example of this is in English youth level football where parents and coaches use what I call 'box-to-box pressure'. If a player has possession in the defensive penalty area, it is common to hear a yell of 'get rid of it!' When someone has the ball in the opponents' penalty area, there's a good chance someone will yell, 'shoot!' This crowd/coach-inflicted pressure leads to an attacking player rushing a decision when in fact they have time, or a defender kicking the ball to the opposition.

What I want to point out is that it is difficult to change a nation's style of play because it has taken years of conditioning to develop. Something absorbed at such a deep level can't simply be rectified by a change of manager or tactics. Deciding whether to pass, shoot or dribble, deciding when to make a move and with which foot and which technique are all important factors in the development of emotional and cognitive skills. Without those skills players can be affected by things like box-to-box pressure which lead to micro panic. This happens at such a deep level that a player will react even if they are in a different environment without box-to-box pressure. It's a result of deep-seated conditioning, just like when you go back to your old school classroom and automatically sit in the chair you used to sit in. You are no longer in school, but you still adhere to the school rules. Football is no different which explains why players still adhered to the old conditioning when the FA brought in foreign managers to create new conditions that would hopefully bring success. The new conditions were being overridden by old conditioning. Change at this level is systematic.

Italian football is more technical than English football. Going on loan from Inter Milan to Charlton Athletic was a struggle at first due to the cultural differences on the pitch. What struck me when moving to England was the changing room environment; it was so different to what I was used to. In England before a match the players would play music, be loud and smile. In Italy we weren't allowed to play music in the changing room. It was silent, it was serious, and it was about concentration before a match.

—**Raffaele Buondonno**
former Inter Milan striker

Losing our artists

Just as players drop out of the system because they feel disillusioned or because they do not meet the conditions, so we also lose creative and technical players who change their style to survive under those same conditions. That's why there are so few creative players in England. Overcoming the culture is really difficult. Growing up in England, I genuinely believed that people who grew up in other countries were better footballers because it was common to hear 'who do you think you are, <insert foreign creative player of the moment here>?' anytime a player tried to express themselves creatively. Creative expectations were limited and passed on like hand-me-downs. Just as kids in school seek praise from their teachers, young players seek praise from their coaches, because the more your coach praises you, the better your chances are of starting in the team, earning a contract and progressing through the system. In short, meeting the conditions leads to meeting your dream as a footballer.

Scott Parker had a very good career, starting at Charlton and earning moves to Chelsea FC, Newcastle United FC, West Ham United FC, Tottenham Hotspur FC, Fulham FC and 18 appearances for the senior England team. Parker started out as a technical player, someone who worked more with the ball than without it and produced brilliant performances doing so, performances that led to him being rated as one of the best young players in the country and representing England youth from Under-16 to Under-21. I remember when Parker was in the Charlton reserves entering the final stage of his rehab and trained with the youth team I was in. Technically he was on another level, on the cusp of the first team. My teammates and I couldn't understand why he wasn't a regular in the first team, in fact, most people in the club couldn't understand. He was rated as one of the best in the country for his age group and a regular for the England youth teams, yet he struggled to hold a regular place in the Premier League new boy's first team. The rumour in the Charlton training ground was that the manager had told Parker he needed to tackle more if wanted to be a regular in the team.

I had the pleasure of playing with Scott Parker from the youth team to reserves and the first team at Charlton Athletic FC. He went from being one of the best number 10s in the country at youth and reserve football, scoring and creating goals on a regular basis, to being one of the best defensive midfielders in the Premier League breaking up the opponents' attack week in, week out.

Parker's transition from number 10 to defensive midfield didn't happen smoothly. While on the brink of the first team, it was difficult for Parker as a number 10 to fit into the 4-4-2 system that the first team played. So our first team manager at the time, Alan Curbishley, told Scott that he needed to be more like Mark Kinsella, a more rounded player that tackles more and is involved in the whole game.

Then former Crystal Palace legend Mark Bright, who was playing for Charlton at the time, took Parker to an Arsenal game. At the game they bumped into former Manchester United legend Paul Ince. Bright told Ince that Parker was the future of Charlton; Ince asked him where he played and Parker replied that he played number 10. 'Number 10?

Number f**king 10? You need to be like me! Running up and down the f**king pitch! Tackling and scoring goals, none of this number 10 rubbish,' was Ince's sharp response.

—**Jonathan Fortune**
former Charlton Athletic FC player

As a result, Parker tackled more, a whole lot more. In fact, his game became all about tackling. He established himself in the Charlton first team and earned moves to some of the biggest clubs in England, along with 18 caps for the national team. How many Scott Parkers have there been in England? I know loads. Players that have either dropped out of the game or changed their game to meet the conditions.

When explaining why it's difficult for a British player to win the *Balon d'Or*, an award traditionally given to the most creative players in the world, former Everton midfielder Leon Osman spoke of the cultural expectations British players have. Osman said that he would not let a British player stand around doing the nice stuff; he would demand that they join in with the team and share the workload, because that's what you're expected to do as a British player. He also explained that when British players work as hard for the team as they are expected to, they lose their flair and all the individual skills they could bring to the game, things that set players apart from the rest.

English football and the business side of the game are evolving more than ever before. Elite clubs in the Premier League are building a strong culture from the academies up. Slowly, club by club, the determination to hold onto the identity and conditions of old is loosening and a more mindful approach is being brought to the fore, either through professional development by the Football Association at St George's Park, or through independent organisations. Clubs are now better equipped to appreciate and unlock talent.

This means that players with diverse talents are being pushed forward, from people like Phil Foden of Manchester City FC to Tashan Oakley Boothe of Tottenham Hotspur FC. They complement each other, which in turn benefits England. Both players were members of the Under-17 World Cup-winning squad.

Changing how the game is seen involves creating new conditions, a new way of judging talent and new expectations for players to meet. I am aware, however, that this education, along with funded services – like the emotional literacy I provide – is currently only for the minority, the Premier League clubs. But it works. I have seen a dramatic shift in consciousness over the years as a result of the extra services the Premier League clubs provide as well as the ideas from overseas managers. For example, Jose Mourinho's influence on the coaches and players he's worked with has been transformational. Liverpool coach Michael Beale has told me how inspirational Mourinho has been, relating stories of their time together at Chelsea during Mourinho's first stint at the club. Drawing attention to how Mourinho refers to football as 'human science', Beale talks mostly about non-footballing moments of magic that Mourinho has created, moments that have inspired coaches to think outside the box.

Behind the contrast in culture

During an interview, former England manager and current Maccabi Tel Aviv coaching consultant Steve McClaren spoke of his time managing Dutch Eridivisie side FC Twente. McClaren was blown away by the fact that Dutch players from the age of nine are educated in football intelligence and that a 21-year-old Twente player spent 20 minutes telling him what he would do tactically against the team in the coming fixture. An impressed McLaren said that no English player would have been able to do that. McLaren has managed the likes of Steven Gerrard, Paul Scholes and Wayne Rooney; I would be surprised if those players didn't have the knowledge to give a 20-minute tactical view of how to approach the coming game, however, being brought up in a system based on command and control may have stopped them from putting their opinions forward.

In his late teens, Tottenham Hotspur's utility man Eric Dier played in Portugal with Sporting and in England with Everton. Although an England international, Dier calls himself a foreigner when it comes to playing football in the English top division. In an interview with *The Guardian* newspaper, Dier gives his definition of a good player, stating that for one thing they would be able to acknowledge mistakes and correct them for themselves, values he learnt growing up in Portugal. Dier describes the contrast between England and Portugal. In Portugal, the coach sits on the bench and doesn't say a word while in England coaches tend to shout at players when they make mistakes and talk them through the game, which takes away their independence and stops them learning from the experience. This is not how all coaches in England behave, but I do agree with Dier that it's common. When I went to Holland to watch Vitesse Arnhem versus Zeeburgia Under-16s in 2015, I remember being shocked at how quiet the managers were on the sideline, especially when the players made mistakes. It just wasn't what I was used to.

Not many people know about Eric Dier's history. He went to Everton on loan from Sporting Lisbon when he was 16, but Everton were not sure about his potential at the time so he returned to Sporting Lisbon where he continued his development before being sold to Tottenham. I watched Eric Dier on numerous occasions, but he wasn't ready for the England

Under-17s as he had some physical issues. When he jumped, his hip flexors rotated so he wasn't staying stable. I spoke about it to David Weir and Alan Stubbs, his coaches at the time.

I remember seeing Dier in a reserve game playing alongside David Weir and doing a great recovery run. I waited for him after the game and said, 'You're ready for England now'. He had quality, but it needed to be nurtured. Adapting to a new style of football is challenging for seasoned professionals let alone a teenager.

We have great young talents who have the same qualities we admire in those across the sea. We have to support those qualities better for them to reach their full potential and for England as a nation to reach its full potential too. That includes people whose qualities are different.

Eric Dier's first game for England was in Slovakia for the Under-18s when I was head coach. I took him and Nathan Redmond to the European finals when they were both a year younger than the others. The rest is history!

—Noel Blake
former England Under-19 head coach

Adaptation was a struggle for Dier. He had to leave Portugal and come to England, two countries with very different conditions. Sometimes being 'good enough' isn't enough. Fortunately, in Blake, Dier had someone who gave him the platform to showcase his talents. Dier had to adapt because he was moving from one country to another, however, the same situation also happens to English players in England.

Why are Brazilians the most skilful?

I did an unofficial survey asking people to say which nation's team in the last 30 years they considered the most skilful. Brazil received 78 per cent of the votes. When I asked these random voters why, their answers included futsal, beach soccer, playing street football and copying the icons that came before them from Zico, Garrincha and Pele to Ronaldo, Ronaldinho and Neymar. It's not surprising most people think the Brazilians are the most skilful, but I don't think it can be explained by just one reason. Brazil's culture creates not only a collective way of thinking, but also a collective way of development.

- **Barefoot**
  A current trend is for sports brands to make barefoot editions of running trainers, the idea being that running barefoot, or as close to barefoot as possible, will strengthen the muscles and ligaments in and around the foot, including the smaller muscles that may not be able to move freely in a traditional shoe. It's not uncommon for Brazilians to play barefoot. This allows their arches to act as natural shock absorbers and activates micro muscles in their feet, ankles, legs and hips improving balance, coordination and proprioception. On the pitch, the relationship between ball and foot is more intimate, creating a variety of touches of the highest standard which can be used in different scenarios.
- **Futsal**
  The name futsal was coined by FIFA and it derives from merging the Spanish words for football (*futból*) and hall (*sala*). Originating on the streets of Uruguay, futsal started because keen football lovers wanted to play football but had nowhere to do it. Futsal is a style of football that is heavily woven into Brazilian culture. It's a five-a-side game, usually played indoors on a small pitch with hockey-sized goals and a size 4-weighted ball. It's a fast-moving game which helps develop touch, agility and speed of thought. The emotional side of the game is continuously exercised too. The players receive the ball under pressure and pass to someone under pressure, thanks to the constant presence

of their opponents, which creates the foundation for other physical skills. Playing at high speed in a limited space requires the highest level of efficiency and physical skills. Players also have to have well developed emotional skills, known in football as 'composure'.

In Australia when I was first introduced to football outdoors, the space was very big. When I was ten years old I was playing on a full-size 11-a-side pitch. The curriculum has changed now with smaller sided games for younger players. All the things they would do three, four or five times in one half of an 11-a-side they now do 15 to 20 times in one half of futsal. This leads to them having to pass, dribble and defend more as well as have more touches and make decisions quicker. It improves first touch, passing and shooting. Those are the positives that futsal can bring to football. The negatives are you don't get to play a pass longer than 20 yards, the game just doesn't present itself that way. Whereas in 11-a-side you can switch the play and play a ball for someone to run onto, in futsal the ball stays on the ground most of the time.

Another advantage of futsal is that everyone has to be an all-rounder, everyone has to attack and everyone has to defend, whereas in football there's more responsibility placed on specific positions. I think this is where Brazil benefits. Futsal is a big part of their culture and so their players are all-rounders who have really learnt from the small-sided game.

If you look at Brazilian defenders, there are a long line of people who have great ability on the ball from Roberto Carlos, Cafu and Lucio to David Luiz, Thiago Silva and Marcelo. This is not unknown in England, just look at Rio Ferdinand, who had really good feet considering the culture and time he came from, but the point is, he was rare. The defenders in Brazil are as skilled with the ball as the attackers. This is important because the defenders are responsible for starting the attack in all football-based games.

—**Daniel Cappellaro**
Balwyn Futsal Club

In futsal, retaining the ball is something valued by everyone because your team is always vulnerable to an immediate attack and it takes a lot of hard work to win the ball back. You are continuously being asked questions. As an attacker you have to make space within a congested area. You cannot boot the ball up the pitch to get out of a tight spot, so you have to work your way out and improvise in order to break free when a pass is not an option. This develops spatial awareness, awareness of others and an understanding of geometry in order to work the angles of passes. You are continuously faced with problems that may not be the same but can be solved using methods from the same resolution pool, which develops situational awareness. Futsal teaches you to become comfortable with the uncomfortable because there is no hiding place. Players who go from the no time and no space of futsal to the time and space available in an 11-a-side match find it easier to operate, freely using skills that have been developed to work in more intense environments.

Futsal requires speed of thought in a small space. It makes problem solving in an eleven-a-side much easier.

—**Bambang Bayu Saptaji**
Vamos FC Mataram and
Indonesian international futsal player

- **Beach Soccer**
  This is a popular sport in Brazil. Playing on a surface that continuously gives way under your feet brings physical challenges but also physical advantages, strengthening the muscles in the feet, calves, hamstrings, quadriceps and hip flexors, as well as improving agility and power. The ball sits in divots on sand, which requires players to think of alternatives to the traditional pass along the floor.

Advanced skills such as flicks, scoops and chips are not seen as showboating in beach soccer, they are part of the basics of the game. If you cannot perform those skills you will not be efficient in beach soccer where a high technical standard is the norm.

Beach soccer requires a high level of technique because the sand is uneven and technique is sometimes the only option to get yourself out of a ditch. When dribbling on sand, a footballer uses all four parts of the foot to shift the ball around which helps develop skills in the use of this all-important tool.

The ball can be played on the floor or in the air; therefore a high level of concentration and decision-making is required when choosing which technique to use at any specific moment. When running with the ball in the air a footballer has to be comfortable using all parts of the body – foot, thigh, chest, shoulder or head to maintain control of the ball and be aware of his surroundings while also deciding on his next move. Football in the Premier League is played on the floor and in the air; therefore I feel it is important for players to be able to control the ball in both situations in a variety of ways. Beach soccer provides an opportunity for development in this area as well as promoting the value of an alternative style of play.

—Aaron Clarke
Arsenal and England beach soccer captain

I believe beach soccer improves technique in a big way. I found touching the ball with my bare feet developed my understanding of where to strike the ball and how.

At England we play a lot of futvolley and table football which can help with touch and understanding of weight of pass and timing.

What I love about beach soccer is that it encourages the spectacular. One of the best Premiership goals of all time was Wayne Rooney's overhead kick for Manchester United in the derby against Manchester City, a typical way of scoring a goal in beach soccer. I believe beach soccer can bring another dimension to a player's game and diversify their learning.

—**Terry Bowes**
former Arsenal FC player,
Arsenal and England beach soccer player/manager

- **Dance**
  This plays a huge role in the history of Brazil. African slaves were brought to Brazil via Portugal, where they were converted to Christianity and forced to worship their God by the Portuguese government. The slaves would then conduct their own religious practices disguised as parties, adding the music and routines that gave birth to Samba. A similar story is true for Capoeira with slaves disguising self-defence in dance. Brazil has also given birth to and adopted Zouk, Lambazouk, Forró, Samba Partido Alto, Samba de Roda, Lundu, Jongo, Baião, Gafiera, Carimbo, Frevo, Coco, Congado, Lambada, Xote, Xaxado, Batuque, Axé, Funk Carioca and more. This explains their passion for dance. From dancing to celebrate their goals to the Rio carnival, Brazilians are not short of a move or two, but how does dance improve their football skills?

I've danced and played football from a young age. By 15 years old, I was playing for Crystal Palace and going to an Italia Conti associate school centre once a week. It was a strain on my body, but I loved it. As I got older and my body's changes began to accelerate, training became harder in dance and football.

After being released by Crystal Palace FC at 16 years old, I was offered a teaching scholarship at Italia Conti, but I turned it down to sign a football scholarship at Crawley Town FC as football was my first love. I was training full-time as a footballer Monday to Friday and playing matches on Saturdays, my only free days were Sundays, so I would attend the Italia Conti's associate school as a hobby. Practising my street dance moves from YouTube tutorials and doing ballet and jazz musical theatre at the Italia Conti associate school for eight-and-a-half hours was quite demanding.

Physically I further developed my core, at the same time deepening my knowledge of and relationship with my body. I was able to more easily coordinate my body within a split second to adjust for the arrival of the ball and so I became better at controlling and striking the ball as it travelled at speed in the air or changed direction in the last moment. Ballet improved my jumps and the arm movement port de bras, where you stand erect, engaging the muscles of your back to display elegance when using your arms, helped me in a big way as a striker when holding off defenders because my foundation (my back) was solid.

On the flipside, my football restricted my dance. The more powerful I became, the more my quads grew. I became over-developed for ballet, restricting my ability to perform some of the basic moves. Various types of dance bring a variety of benefits to footballers. You condition your physique in a different way, forming relationships with parts of your body and using muscles that you wouldn't normally use. You then use these new skills in performance on the pitch without even thinking about it.

—**Cecil Thomas**
former Crawley Town player who holds a Diploma in
Performing Arts from the Italia Conti Arts Centre

We have over 600 muscles in our body and co-ordinating all of them rhythmically is a skill, as I mentioned in the chapter on unconscious competence. A Brazilian player rhythmically coordinates his 600-plus muscles to dance with the opponent, leading them into a false sense of security. They perform a kind of footballing salsa: taking the lead, creating a feedback loop and breaking the pattern at the last minute to break free and progress past their opponent. Just like dance, the best at performing skills are those who react to what happens in the here and now, going with the flow and letting their body become at one with the music. Ronaldo Lima, Ronaldinho, Robinho and Neymar are the kings of one-on-one situations. There are thousands of Brazilian players who do not quite make it to that level of football, but they all have similar qualities.

I have found that during training Brazilians need to rehearse; they need time to be playful with the ball. You can't train like you do in England. There needs to be a time to just have love for the game, to have the ball and just practise things. When you think about it, it's the skill you learnt as kids from peers or by playing with ball, no coaches taught you it. The skill of improvisation. The things I saw during my time at Sao Paolo when we played small-sided games absolutely blew my mind!

They didn't just want football; they needed it. Poverty, violence and drugs are big problems in Brazil. The only way to get yourself out is football because if you don't, the only jobs available are jobs in hotels. That won't get you out of the favela. There's a need to be a football player and that need outweighs the want that we have. Don't get me wrong, I do think that people like John Terry, Steven Gerard and Wayne Rooney needed to be players, but I'm referring to the general population. I thought I needed to be a football player, but I knew that if I wasn't, I could go and work for my dad or I could be a postman, there were more options for me. But for those kids in Brazil there's not many options. That creates a whole other level of motivation.

In Brazil you cannot make a negative substitution ever! If you take off a number ten or a number nine you will get whistled at. Brazilian football is only for attacking and creative players; that is the only thing they value. Working hard in Brazilian football is based more on technical excellence. In England we see working hard as crashing through two tackles.

Culture plays a big part in football and in Brazil theirs is clear with everyone pulling in the same direction.

—**Micheal Beale**
former Sao Paolo assistant manager, Chelsea youth coach and current Liverpool youth coach

Being

Growing up in England I felt that there was an emphasis on being serious in football. Banter happens, but generally you get judged if you're seen to be mucking around even when not within the professional space. When I was in Berlin for the 2015 Barcelona versus Juventus Champions League final, I was speaking to a local in my hotel the day before the game and he was showing me pictures from the internet of Neymar and Dani Alves clowning on the escalator in a place that looked like an airport or train station. I thought to myself, *they are going to play a Champions League final and look at them! They are either extremely relaxed or this is how they manage the low-level anxiety that many experience before a game.* Either way, they were allowed to experience it. Brilliant! On the pitch, as Beale mentioned, they seriously went about their business, creatively carving out a win, with Neymar getting the last goal of the 3 - 1 victory.

This is not to say that all Brazilians play futsal and beach soccer, go barefoot and love to dance. It is just to highlight the key elements of their culture because it affects everything. Rehearsals are part of their programme so there's less resistance to players performing skills during a match, it's seen as a natural progression and something that players, coaches and fans value.

Brazil has been an eye-opener for me; it's all about what you can do with the ball. Before training on Fridays, before Saturday's game we have this thing called Rachão. During Rachão the players flick the ball over each other's heads and do skills out of this world! Also, we have a foot table – a ping-pong table that you use to play two-touch football. The players are doing bicycle kicks, jumping on the table using different parts of the body to slam the ball on the other side of the table. The guys over here make a game out of anything. There's a cooler box at the training ground, they play two-touch on the cooler box. I think that this is part of the culture from their younger years of not having any money, so they would make games out of things in their environment.

The coaches here do not micromanage the players, they leave them to be who they are gonna be. They give them knowledge to develop their football intelligence based on who they are. Everything the coaches add here is to support who the players are. In England, if I toe punted a ball everyone would laugh. In Brazil, they would rate me for being innovative and acknowledging that I didn't have time to side foot the ball or use my laces so I came up with another idea. I scored a goal with my chest for Corinthians to win the league and the attention I got for it was unreal. My idol Ronaldo Luis Nazário de Lima came up to me to shake my hand. In England, they would have asked me why didn't I head it. I've played for the top clubs in seven different countries and I've seen how they treat kids who come from different backgrounds. They look for the talent they have and don't try to change it.

—**Colin Kazim-Richards**
Corinthians and Turkey international

There is a tremendous amount to be learnt from another country's culture from the beliefs and values of its people. Players and coaches with international experience are at a great advantage because they can compare and contrast, absorbing the best bits from the culture they are immersed in. Understanding the role culture plays in football and explaining the importance to players is vital to their ongoing education.

Another crucial part of education is an understanding of mental health — and that is what we're going to look at next. We'll look at examples of how players manage their thinking and reactions in a positive way. We'll also discuss 'lower level' mental illness topics not usually seen as threatening, such as addiction and depression, which affect a large number of players and which have the potential to cause more serious problems.

FIVE

MENTAL HEALTH

It was 2009, I was playing for Charlton Athletic at the time and I was injured again. I remember sitting on the treatment table and bursting into tears, people were just walking past me as I sat there crying uncontrollably. I went back to my hotel room and took some pills in an effort to overdose and take my own life. I woke up in the hospital after my failed suicide attempt; it's probably the only time I can look back with such happiness at failing at something. Yet I went into training the next day as though nothing happened.

Looking back, I don't think people knew what to say to a grown man sitting there sobbing on the treatment table, it probably made them uncomfortable. But it's a big problem in a team sport if a player feels so alone at their lowest point. It's those kind of situations that motivate me now. I wouldn't want anybody else to be in the position I was in and have people walking past them as though they weren't there.

—**Leon McKenzie**
Former Crystal Palace striker
and Super Middleweight professional boxer

There has been a lot of talk about mental health in recent years. Football has had to take a long hard look at how it handles the subject because of the number of cases that have made the news.

The term 'mental health' describes a person's psychological and emotional condition. This psycho-emotional condition plays a pivotal role in how they experience the world around them, both the good and the bad.

Depression, anxiety, addiction and panic attacks are often described in the media as mental health instead of mental illness issues. This basic misunderstanding increases the risk of ill health and means people are unable to identify subtle warning signs in others or, in Leon's case, much clearer signs.

Commonly, low-level mental health issues can arise out of everyday activities like exams, running late, interviews, anticipating arguments, looking at bank statements or waiting for news. I describe these scenarios as 'low level' because, more often than not, people will be able to go about their day as usual after the stressful experience is over. For some people, however, those situations can develop into high-level mental health problems, leaving them feeling so bad they may not even want to leave their bed. In other words, the extent to which people experience the problem is dependent on how it makes them feel. Many people involved in performance – actors before they walk on stage, CEOs before going into an important meeting, footballers as they walk onto the pitch – talk of being a little anxious and how it helps them to focus. Acknowledging, understanding and managing feelings can change the game.

The banter cycle

Banter and practical jokes play a prominent role in football. It's how a player survives the furnace of pressure, prevents themselves from being the victim of somebody else's teasing and counters the boredom of waiting around at training grounds and airports.

The joking around that happens at football clubs is miles outside the boundaries found in other professional environments. There isn't much some players wouldn't do for a laugh: like a young professional squatting on top of the toilet and catching his poo to use against his team mates, or a 12-year-old player secretly peeing in his teammate's Lucozade bottle and then watching him drink it. Everyone accepts it on the surface, but how does it really affect people?

I go to clubs around the country presenting a programme called The Grey Area which covers the differences between banter and bullying. No matter the league, age group or part of the country, when I ask people if they've ever been angry, upset, sad or if their performance has been negatively affected as a result of banter, the response is almost always the same: 'I'm cool,' or 'we're cool.'

There are players that love the banter but there are players that hate it too. Eventually, someone in the pack will say something which gives me an insight into what really goes on in the changing room. As soon as they do, I home in and explore, and that's when they begin to open up, sharing the comments that are made and their opinions of them. Words like 'frustration', 'anger', 'loss of confidence' and 'stress' come up a lot when victims of 'The Banter Cycle' describe the effect banter has had on their personal and professional lives.

Because banter is a playful way of teasing it is often difficult to see when it crosses the line and offends someone. While some topics are seen as obvious no-go areas, the only person who can truly judge whether the banter is offensive or not is the person it's being directed at. Why don't the ones that hate it say anything? Often, it's because once a player does build up the courage to talk about how he is negatively affected by banter, his teammates laugh at him. No wonder people stay silent; they're going to be laughed at if they say something and laughed at if they don't! It's very common that when a player shares in session that they have been negatively affected by the banter happening in their changing room, it is the first time the person's teammates have had any idea how they feel about it.

I was one of the main perpetrators when it came to the banter. I would set it up and then everyone would join in and off it went. When I was at Wimbledon FC (pre-AFC Wimbledon) we were called The Crazy Gang because the stuff that we did was crazy – if there were limits, I didn't see them. With characters like Vinnie Jones and John Fashanu around, aggression was high, and the banter was intense. We were reckless; there weren't too many hotels that would take our squad for our away games!

The press would come to our training ground and try to dominate, so we told them that they were safe on the concrete but once they stepped onto the grass we couldn't be held responsible for what happened to them. One day, a man from one of the top newspapers overstepped the mark and came onto the pitch with his camera crew. He got a warning, but he ignored it, so the bucket of blackcurrant juice that the players used to drink from ended up all over him – and £20,000 worth of camera equipment.

One day we had a team meeting with a sports psychologist about banter in our changing room and one player told the team that it really affected him when we spoke about his mum, to the stage where he didn't want to come into training. He had a young-looking mum, so players would say inappropriate things. I could relate because my mum looked young too, in fact in my younger years I told my mum to stop coming to my games and that she couldn't come back to watch me play until she had grey hair on her head, that was my way of dealing with it. The young player at Wimbledon spoke up and the team listened, and from then on the jokes stopped. He had a lot of talent and went on to have a good career.

Banter can make or break you. I've seen it become too much for players, it makes them feel as though they aren't accepted so they isolate themselves and don't bond with the group. Ultimately, this is the price they pay for staying at the club.

—**Marcus Gayle**
former Wimbledon and Jamaica international

The intention of banter is innocent, but that doesn't mean that what is said and done doesn't have a negative effect on the receiver. However, social and relational bullying is often dressed up as banter. When you are in a group, that group has the power to have an impact on your mental health, as Marcus talked about earlier. Social and relational bullies use the power of the group against their victims to highlight their mistakes or insecurities and laugh at them. Banter and social and relational bullying both have the same pattern, hence it can be difficult to detect at times.

True feelings

'So!' I say as I pump myself up for another emotionally intense session. 'Who gets angry, upset or sad as a result of the banter that happens here?' I'm at a northern Premier League club in a room full of 12-year-olds. The chorus rings around the room. 'I'm cool', 'we're cool', 'we used to have a problem, but it's sorted', 'we're cool'. I begin to pace up and down as I throw out some examples to the room, my eyes scan each player's face, locking in for two to three seconds. Some look at the floor, some shrug off the questions and then, bingo! Everyone turns to look at the boy with his hand up at the back of the room, his face wearing the same expression it has had since I walked in the room. The room is silent. I signal for him to speak. The floodgates open up and he starts wailing; he is inconsolable and has to be taken out of the room. That is the catalyst for the group to tell their truth. I cannot tell you the details of the story, but it's an example of the power the group holds. Millions dream of being a footballer at a Premier League club, yet I meet players in Premier League teams who do not want to be there because of how their teammates make them feel.

The ref blows the whistle for kick-off. One second. The ball gets sent back to me. Two seconds. Bang! I smash the ball towards the goal from the halfway line. Three seconds. The ball is zipping through the sky. Four seconds. The ball lobs the goalkeeper and lands in the back of the net. My name is etched in the Guinness Book of World Records for the fastest ever cup final strike: 4.2 seconds.

At the time of my record-breaking strike for my school, Ernest Bevin, at Arsenal's Highbury football ground, I was playing for Charlton Athletic FC but it wasn't long till Tottenham Hotspur bought me for £450,000 and that's when the problems started. My teammates had no problem with me being bought for a six-figure sum or that I earned a lot of money, but I couldn't say the same about my youth team manager. I was getting paid more than him and he made it known that he was not happy with it. Whenever I made a mistake he would turn to my teammates on the bench and say, 'He shouldn't be getting that kind of money'. It was bad enough that he was saying it, but what was he trying to do? Turn my teammates against me? He is an adult and I was just a kid. He was supposed to be looking after me and nurturing my career, instead he became another hurdle. I had to go into training every day knowing that these were the things he was saying about me. It knocked my confidence.

My manager was a former Spurs player. He was an unbelievable coach in terms of putting sessions together, but I feel he let his emotions get in the way of his job. His son was at Spurs before me and played the same position, so when the club bought me, he took it personally and I was more than aware of that. I was 14 and didn't know how to deal with the treatment. My back was up and my attitude changed, I became very angry.

When I became too old to play in the youth team, I thought that I had left the politics of the father–son set up behind me, only to find the same problem in the reserves with my manager, another former Spurs player. When I was in the youth team, his son had come on trial, which I thought was strange at the time, because he had previously played for a second league club you don't go on trial to Spurs from a club like that.

Anyway, because he had no say over what happened in the youth team, once the trial ended, his son wasn't signed up. I thought that was the end of that situation, but it was only the beginning.

On my 18th birthday I broke my leg. Everyone was asking how I was doing and when would I be back playing. Everyone, that is, except my manager. What I didn't realise was that his son was coming back to Spurs and now that his father was the manager, he was certain to get signed. This is exactly what happened, and he went on to play ahead of me. It all started to make sense.

The stress of continuously fighting losing battles took their toll and looking back, I cannot believe what I went through. My time at Spurs should have been about me trying to earn a career; instead I was victim to two men trying their best to continue their legacy at the club, to my detriment. My last season at Spurs came when first team manager Jacques Santini, who had begun to show faith in me one pre-season, was sacked and replaced by Martin Jol who signed Aaron Lennon and Wayne Routledge, two young players who played in my position and cost a lot more than me. That's when I made the decision to leave with one year remaining on my contract. The weight was off my shoulders. I felt good, I felt free.

—**Owen Price**
former Tottenham Hotspur winger

Tips for managing banter and social and relational bullying

- **Honesty:** People will innocently offend you if you do not tell them that you are offended. It is good to let them know you don't like it, but there is another advantage. If the person continues to behave in this way and you have to report them, then the fact you have already talked about it to them will add clarity to your complaint.
- **Identity:** Try to avoid jokes about identity. Steering away from a person's identity doesn't mean you will not offend

them, but it will reduce the chances because other topics are likely to be less personal.
- **Boundaries:** Discuss boundaries.
- **Ownership:** Own your mistakes. If you offend someone, apologise so it becomes easier to move forward.
- **Team Representative:** This person will assess the banter in the group, chair discussions on incidents that may appear to be social and relational bullying, and report to manager if need be. If the manager is the problem, then seek advice from governing bodies.

Players can discuss the above points among themselves and staff can use them in skilled small talk during times of intimacy, for example when walking from the training pitch into the building.

Problems, pressure and performance anxiety

Players feel pressure from their parents, friends, coaches, club owners, media and fans, and the pressure either is managed effectively by the players and their support system or it isn't, and the pressure manifests.

If I have problems in my relationship or with my family this will have a terrible effect on my performance. I have to be 100 per cent clear in my mind when I start a game.

Football doesn't educate us on the link between us as a person and us as a player, more attention should be placed on mental health. Unfortunately, the consensus is 'they make a lot of money and don't even work hard, what problems do they have? The tough decision of which car to buy?' as though money is the medication to our problems. This type of thinking only isolates the player.

Because of social media you cannot get away from people, so a player can get shouted at in real life and then get negative comments on their social media accounts. It's sad that this type of behaviour is accepted as normal, especially when people would not accept this type of behaviour in their own workplace.

There are three things I do when I feel down:

1. *I live in Eindhoven but my family lives in Amersfoort. When I feel down I go to my hometown of Amersfoort to hang out with my family and friends, talking with them is my therapy.*
2. *When I feel down my confidence on the pitch gets low. Other than visiting my friends and family, I use training to springboard my confidence back into a positive place which transfers into my matches.*
3. *Sjors Ultee, who is the assistant coach at FC Utrecht, was like a mental health coach for me. He was always on hand to help me and when I felt bad, I always felt that I could call on him when I needed him and he'd be there to help me. Although I no longer play at Utrecht, I know he's only a call away.*

—**Bart Ramselaar**
PSV Eindhoven and Holland international

Some players get a motivational buzz from pressure and others falter, their wellbeing paying the price. Players have various strategies for managing pressure. Some play golf as they find it therapeutic, others do the same as Bart and go back to visit family and friends. However, some find the pressure of professional football and life in general too much to handle, so they escape by partying, drinking excessive amounts and gambling, which can then cause additional problems in their personal lives and on the pitch; problems that plague football.

I caught up with former Arsenal and Manchester City player Gael Clichy who told me about his spiritual journey, a way of being that improved the quality of his life off the pitch, which in turn improved his life on the pitch.

When I had my daughter I realised that life is more than football. It changed my perspective on the whole, and stopped me being sad during the week because we lost a game or because I performed badly. The game really took over my life!

For the last six years I have been meditating regularly using Yoga Nidra. Yoga Nidra is a meditation that helps me to block out the negative self-talk, encourage positive thoughts and helps me focus. Like all players I had a time when I had difficult moments where my performances dipped, and I began to overthink situations. I've seen extremely talented players fail because they spend their mental energy worrying about what could potentially go wrong, instead of thinking what could go right and enjoying themselves. I was lucky enough to be part of the 'Invincibles' that went the season unbeaten, playing alongside people like Dennis Bergkamp. I learnt that football is just a game, of course I have a duty and a responsibility to perform but this doesn't take away from the fact that it is just a game. If you lose a game, then so what, you lose a game. Three days later you have a chance to win a game. I was surrounded by people like Patrick Vieira who had nothing to prove to anybody; they resiliently played the game, whether they did good or bad they applied themselves the same way, they just played the game. I learnt from them at a young age how to manage my emotional condition.

Cristiano Ronaldo and Lionel Messi have good control of self, if they miss a penalty it's not a problem as they believe that they have the ability to score afterwards, because that's who they are. Not everybody has this quality but those who do are top players. Being able to block out the negative noise and negative self-talk is a skill in itself.

I feel that meditation connects me to the game more. I started when I was at Arsenal. During the early stages of practising meditation, I played against Barcelona and I had an excellent game, my mindset was different and I felt so good. Before I began meditating, I remember someone saying to me you can train as hard as you want physically, learn as much as you want tactically but to make a bigger difference you must train the brain. At the time I didn't think too much about it because I was young and thought I was a good player, so I only focused on playing the game. After I started Yoga Nidra I decided that I am going to travel more, meet different people and experience life.

When I first arrived at Arsenal I was only 17 and I wasn't aware of what football could bring. I found it difficult moving from France to England because I was going to a country where I couldn't speak the language and being without my family. The pitch was therapy to me as it was a place I spoke the same language as everybody else; didn't think about anything else except the game and I was loving it. Training with the likes of Robert Pires, Patrick Vieira and Sol Campbell was like being in a different world, I was so happy to be there. I just played with the belief I could beat anyone.

The first season I played at Arsenal was the easiest one, because no one knew who I was and no one was expecting me to perform to a great level. I got to discover myself as a player and nurture my ability. During this time, I had a football innocence, a fearless factor, and didn't think too deep into football until after my first year at Arsenal people began to class me as one of the better players, then I realised that I had to perform to the highest standard every moment to be successful and began to focus more. The moment I paid attention to playing in front of 80,000 people and feeling the expectation that came with my wages, I felt the need to justify my position and my earnings.

The pressure can be intense, people are counting on you to perform week in, week out and this is where you lose players from the game. I've seen many falter. They have the physical qualities but not the mental qualities to sustain their career, whether it be playing at the top of football or playing in the game at all. Five years after arriving at Arsenal was a big moment in my career, Ashley Cole had just signed for Chelsea and now Arsene Wenger and the fans had invested a huge amount of trust in me to perform every three days.

Although I moved to a team and league that played a higher standard of football, the biggest challenge was adapting to a new country. Little things like cooking food, paying bills and trying to find things in Sainsbury's or Tesco, difficult things when you cannot read or speak the same language of those around you. Arsenal were very good in the support they provided, but there's only so much the club can do. I was also lucky to have the likes of Thierry Henry, Patrick Vieira, Jeremie Aliadere, Mathieu Flamini, Robert Pires and other people that spoke French in the team.

Ego is a big thing in football. The best managers know how to manage egos, but bigger than the ego is managing the person as a whole. I've had the opportunity to train under Arsene Wenger and Pep Guardiola, both of whom I class as football geniuses. They tell you and teach you in great detail how to see out situations on the pitch, so the group works well as one. This is important so that people do not do their own thing. When a player is earning astronomical amounts of money, it's difficult to tell him that he isn't playing well. If he's not playing well, he needs to hear that he's not playing well.

I am currently reading Ego is the Enemy, a book that, if I were to become a manager one day, I would get my players to read it because teams have diverse personalities. Without the leadership from the coaching staff and the players themselves, it can become difficult for the more humble players to express themselves within the group, leading to them being overshadowed by the ego of others, off and on the pitch with some players taking advantage of others. It's not exactly bullying, but the contrast of personalities leads some to be the victims of the others. Because of this, it's important to make life easier for young players by educating them so they can build themselves up to handle what football and life throw at them. So many positive things happen as a result of being a footballer – you're gonna be famous, invited to parties, be able to buy whatever you want for yourself, family and friends – but with all this comes so much negativity. If you're not strong mentally you'll crash into a brick wall.

Lastly, feedback in football can be better, approaching a player with love and care, telling him, 'Come one we need you, you're an important player, how you're performing isn't great but it isn't too bad either.' This is important. Now that more money is in the game, the care for the person isn't there as much as it should be, and the egos are growing out of control. Meditation helped me appreciate the things that make me human a whole lot more. I always want to win and paying attention to my personal development helps me win on and off the field.

—**Gael Clichy**
former Arsenal and France international

Performance anxiety is the fear of having to perform in front of an audience. It's also known as stage fright. The reasons footballers suffer from performance anxiety and how it manifests itself can vary from player to player, but one common behaviour is for someone to second-guess themselves in a match. They may avoid getting the ball by strategically hiding on the pitch, and when they do find themselves in possession they choose the easier and less risky option of passing backwards, sideways or kicking the ball up the field. When defending, they take up positions that make them less vulnerable. A defender may sit deep because they don't want the striker to run in behind them. Although this doesn't sound so bad, by doing so the player has extended the pitch, making their teammates vulnerable because they have just created more space for the opponents to play in.

Performance anxiety creates a distortion of reality. A player's key skill (decision-making) starts working from diluted information, which in turn dilutes the level of their performance.

Players develop performance anxiety in different ways, for example a youngster trying to break into the first team or a senior player trying to get into the starting line-up may become anxious because of the pressure they place on themselves to prove their worth. Wanting something so badly can lead to self-doubt, indecision and fear of failure, which leads to trying to do things to perfection. For example, instead of shooting when he has sight of the target, an anxious striker trying to show his worth may take extra touches to set the ball up perfectly to rule out a potential block from the defender, or set the ball up for a clean strike.

Sometimes it's pressure. Whether it's a professional match or a Sunday league match, matches are taken seriously. It doesn't matter if the pressure is from others or what the player places on themselves, it can lead to anxiety.

My thoughts and emotions have a huge effect on my performance. When I have a lot of things on my mind like, 'What does the coach think of me?' or 'If I do this or that will I be able to play the full 90 minutes?' These things worry me and have a negative effect on how I play.

—**Bart Ramselaar**
PSV Eindhoven and Holland international

Lack of communication leads to players struggling to make sense of what is going on around them. As we have mentioned before, something as simple as a training game or shadow play can cause anxiety when players assume that one team is really the starting 11 for the next official match and the other team (the team they are in) didn't make the starting line-up and therefore won't be starting the next official match.

Sometimes all a player needs to hear is the reason why they are not being selected. At other times a player will be told why they are not in the team but will struggle to handle not being needed at that time. Managing rejection is a struggle that can ruin careers. Players don't come forward and actually say they are upset or feel hurt, but tell you in other ways, one of the main ones being, 'I'm leaving this club'. Most of the time they don't leave, they just need to vent, but I did know a player who moved clubs quite often because he fell out with the managers. The style of play may not have been to his liking, but did he need to fall out with them to get his point across? Whenever he saw that he was about to be dropped, or was dropped, he caused an argument.

He struggled with rejection so if he wasn't going to play or sign a new deal or his loan was going to be terminated, he wanted to make sure it was on his terms, i.e. because he wanted to leave and not because the club didn't want him.

Performance anxiety is a phase for some players, others build their identity around it and some struggle to demonstrate their true abilities during an actual game. My friends and I coined the term Training Ground International, also known as TGI, for those who trained like a top international footballer during the week, only to play like an intern on a Saturday.

What is going on within these players? They obviously have the talent – they show it in training, but they struggle to access these skills in an official game because of psycho-emotional stumbling blocks. This happens over and over, whether in the Premier League or a Sunday league. Coaching staff are not trained to manage these scenarios, so a talented player is wrongly labelled as untalented, and then they're not needed any more.

Pressure goes a step past performance. Former Brentford striker Gavin Tomlin is someone I grew up with – we played together in primary school teams, Sunday league teams and semi-professional teams. I remember when we were playing for Staines Town. About 30 seconds before kick-off we would deliberate over the sequence we were about to do. Twenty seconds before kick-off Gavin would walk towards the centre circle to take the kick-off and – "Bluhhhhh!" – throw up. This happened three times out of five, so I asked Gavin what was going on. He said that he didn't know; it was just something he did before most games, like an unconscious ritual almost. I asked him if he was nervous, but he said no. Whatever it was, when he was about to play a match something chemically changed within him.

My first time at a professional football club was when I was

14 and went to Charlton Athletic on trial. And a trial it was. I struggled to be the best version of myself. I was hoping to do something good in return for praise and acknowledgement, a transaction to support my emotional needs. I hoped that any approval I got would give power to my performance and that the effect would snowball.

But the praise and acknowledgement never came. The resulting performance anxiety and insecurity led to me becoming a shadow of myself. I did OK in matches, but not as well as I did in training because the pressure of the game affected the amount and type of calculated risks I was willing to take. Not only was I aware that a mistake would be costly, I was also aware that the judgement of my trial hinged on my performances in the game. Pressure. Needless to say, 'OK' was not good enough to be signed. Keeping my performances safe safely got me released.

Some managers naturally have skills when engaging with others. For those that don't, developing them can be as important as having a sports psychologist on site, maybe more so. I spoke to former Tottenham Hotspur and England defender Anthony Gardner about his career, from being a schoolboy at Port Vale to his England debut. Gardner said there was pressure playing in the Port Vale academy and being promoted into their first team at the age of 17, but he had no problem handling it because he was confident in his ability. However, things changed when he went to Spurs.

I was in Port Vale's academy with my cousin, someone who was on the same level as me with regards to physical and technical ability, but mentally that's where we were different. He couldn't take any form of criticism, whether it be undiluted harsh criticism or constructive criticism, whereas I would get criticised and either take it on board or aim to prove the coach wrong. I don't know where my mindset came from, but I was lucky enough to have it to deal with the pressures that come with playing in this dog-eat-dog sport.

At youth team level we were fragile and invested all our trust in the club and its staff. We were in the transition stage – no longer boys, but not really men yet. A lot of boys can go into their shell in this lost space. It's a space where you are trying to form your identity as a player under intense pressure which you are expected to just deal with.

When I look back, there were talented players that were in my Port Vale youth team that didn't make it. Football ability wasn't their downfall; it was partly down to coaches. Players are fragile, right on the edge, and the coaching styles I've seen either uplift players or send them over the edge.

Coaches are able to coach teenagers to kick a ball but they are not qualified to manage the person. The pressure and the personal problems the kids are going through are hard. I know because I've seen it and I've experienced it. A coach may have gone through their own struggles during their time as a young player, but can they identify the problems that show up in a different form? Can they relate to the young player? Some can and some can't, and those who can't cause great stress for those in their care.

There's a huge void in the development of the person. When I look back on my days in the youth team at Port Vale, if I'd had emotional education about everything that came as part of the game, I would have been in a better state when I was playing. I would have had a better career and been better equipped to manage the big moments that occurred when I played for Tottenham Hotspur FC. The emotional side gets buried because it's seen as weak to show your emotions.

When I was in the bubble of football, there were no disclosures about feelings, it was just pure banter, it wasn't a real environment. During my career I only spoke about my emotions once when I saw a psychiatrist, other than that never, not with my managers or with my teammates. In a game where there are emotional rollercoasters daily, we didn't discuss how we felt, not a word. I wanted to have conversations about my injuries – I needed to tell someone how they affected me, and I needed reassurance. I needed to speak to someone regarding my personal issues around my ex-girlfriend and my mum, I wanted to speak to somebody that I could trust who wasn't that close to me.

Playing in the first team at Port Vale at 17 years old brought a lot of pressure. Physically I was starting to show my potential but mentally I wasn't ready. If you're not a confident person, the emotional side of the game will hamper you. If a player is confidant or borderline arrogant, what I refer to as 'football arrogance' they are better prepared to deal with the pressures of the game.

I had just finished the first half of my second season, so I had been playing in the first team about a year. I knew I was doing well because I was playing every week and getting good reviews. Then one day I was driving home and I got a call from the manager Brian Horton. He said that I had to come back to the stadium right away. Once I got back to the stadium, he told me that the club had received a bid for me and that I was going to Tottenham Hotspur FC. He didn't ask me if I wanted to go; he told me that I was going. He then proceeded to tell me that I needed to go as the club needed money and that it would be a good move for me. Usually when someone of a higher rank like a manager told me to do something I would do it with no questions, but I wanted to know what my options were, so I asked if there were other clubs interested. Horton went on to tell me that Chelsea, Coventry and Liverpool were, but the deal had been done and that I was going to Tottenham!

I transferred for a million pounds. Teenagers didn't really go for a million pounds back then. At the age of 18, I experienced the most difficult six months of my life, going from a town like Staffordshire where I grew up, to London. Neither my agent nor the club helped me to get a place to live. I had only been to London to play matches and now I was living in a hotel. This affected me in a bad way and had a negative impact on how I trained and played. It was a reporter that offered to show me around the area near to the Spurs training ground that helped me find somewhere to live.

I couldn't wait to get back to the Midlands. Every Saturday after the first team had played at home, I would jump in my car and drive up to the Midlands and come back down on Sunday at midnight. I did this for six months. After six months it all came together – I bought a house, I was in the first team and I was more integrated within the team and that's when things changed.

Playing in the first team exposed me to a whole new realm of pressure, pressure that no one had warned me about or prepped me for. I think the players that had been there longer than me had better relationships with the coaches, but as someone who had not been there long and was young and inexperienced, I was looking for others to guide me, whether the older players or the coaching staff. The older players would ask how I was settling in, but at the end of the day they had their own pressures.

My experience taught me that when moving into the Premier League young players need all the support they can get. They need someone in welfare that will help them inside and outside football, someone who is brave enough to challenge in the name of the player's welfare. Players get mental problems for various reasons. Some of those reasons come from playing on the field, injuries are an example – the mental problems that arise from injuries are not dealt with at the time.

Injuries played too big a role in my career for my liking. What I was there to do was taken away from me. On top of that, I felt the pressure from the manager who wanted to see me on the pitch and the fans who also wanted to see me on the pitch. Managers don't have the time to manage these kinds of problems because they are under so much pressure themselves. This is how emotional problems start and they can soon progress into dangerous behaviour patterns as players seek comfort to mask the fact that they can't play or perform at the level expected of them. People deal with this type of pressure and emotional discomfort in different ways, some talk about it and others, like myself, just lock it up inside.

I didn't express how hard I found it to get injured and then not be able to play. The feelings built up inside until they got unleashed in a destructive way – alcohol. I would go drinking to take my mind away from the stresses of my normal routine. I would play every week, get a bad injury, then my wife at the time would have to comfort me. The more that it happened over the years, the more it changed me as a person. It put a strain on my marriage and that's when the search for comfort and distraction began to take my focus away. I kept breaking down during rehab so I began to carry out vices that were quite extreme. One moment I was on a high, playing at Old Trafford, then I would break down and be out for a long time.

When I was injured I wasn't the best of souls to be around. This is a time when players slip into a form of depression, looking for answers and there's no one to speak to. When I got called up to play for England I was on a high, playing week in, week out and fit, missing only two league games that season. My confidence was high, and it was no coincidence that staying fit resulted in me playing my best season I've ever played in the Premier League. Getting called up for my country brought a new pressure, but a good pressure, the type of pressure that comes with an expectation born out of respect, not too much but enough to keep you on your toes.

Eventually when I left Spurs I felt freer. I thought I had been there too long and needed to play more. I transferred from Spurs to Hull City FC and my role as a player changed as I instantly felt that I had more responsibility. I went there as a senior player and was looked upon as a leader. The manager told me that I was one of the main players, whereas at Spurs I hadn't been one of the first names on the team sheet, I was a squad player, which is a whole different realm.

I felt this was now the time to impose myself as a person and although I did have some injury problems while there, generally I felt better within myself. I enjoyed my football a lot more and there was less pressure. Playing at a club like Spurs brings its own pressure; the top five Premier League teams bring a different level of pressure compared with the mid-table Premier League teams. When I was at Spurs I saw players crumble under pressure and so did I. It grabs hold of you and restricts your performance. If I had had support in handling pressure I would have been a better player and Spurs would have seen me as a better player, for sure.

I never spoke about the mental side of the game until my late twenties or early thirties, not one conversation. That's too late.

During the latter part of my career I played for Sheffield Wednesday and teamed up with Jermaine Johnson. I thought, 'oh my God, what a talent! How has this guy never played in the Premier League?' After a month I saw that his application, how he dealt with pressure and his stubbornness were the reasons why he didn't make it to the Premier League. He couldn't control his emotions, which led to him lashing out, getting sent off and so on. There was no one willing to work with him on those things to get the best out of him for the team and for himself. By the time I played with him he was in his early thirties, so it may have been too late by then, but if someone had helped him with his application, how to manage pressure and how to handle criticism five or six years earlier, there is no telling what type of player he would have become. He needed someone to support him in understanding himself more. Jermaine's mind wasn't right, if it had been as agile as his body, his career would have been completely different. Controlling the ball is one thing, controlling your emotions is another.

The other Jermaine I played with at Spurs, Jermaine Defoe, was at the other end of the scale – very serious and very focused. You can't be as consistent as Defoe has been over the years without the right application. There are many players like Jermaine Johnson out there who, with a little extra help, could be something special. Clubs throw away millions every year by not maximising the talent they already have. If they invested a fraction of what they spend on transfers in supporting the talent they already have, not only would they save millions they would create a great team from a group of people that feel valued and indebted to those who have taken the time out to invest in their wellbeing.

—**Anthony Gardner**
former Tottenham Hotspur and England international

Injured heart, injured mind

At football clubs, players develop their body to move efficiently, to prevent injury and to recover from injury, strengthening muscles, increasing flexibility and mobility. The physical is taken care of, but the mind is neglected. Exercising the mind before problems arise and after they occur offers similar benefits to physical exercise. It might be through yoga, which helps you be present in the moment, develops resilience to negative thoughts and improves your overall wellbeing to give you a good foundation for performance personally and professionally. Exercising the mind allows players to manage information, and not be managed by situations. Rehab of the mind helps to overcome the psychological problems that come with injury along with the trauma from the snaps, breaks and pulls. If players had a better understanding of self, they would be able to manage a host of situations better before they become problems.

At the beginning of the 2017/18 Premier League season, Barcelona FC made their interest in Liverpool FC's Philippe Coutinho known. Although Coutinho had a back injury, Barcelona were trying to buy him to replace his international teammate Neymar after he left Barcelona for Paris Saint Germain in a record-breaking £198 million deal. In an attempt to force through the transfer, Coutinho handed in a transfer request but Liverpool made it clear they were not going to sell. Typically, players become 'injured' when they want to leave a club, or a club says their player is injured when they try to offload them, so that the player avoids actually being injured and scuppering the potential transfer. Liverpool fans thought Coutinho was refusing to play in case he became injured and they made their feelings clear on social media.

After days of Coutinho's potential transfer being in the papers, his good friend and Fluminense club doctor Michael Simoni reported that Coutinho was in perfect physical condition to play but not in good psycho-emotional condition. Simoni went on to describe how Coutinho's transfer saga had led to him feeling stressed and anxious, and how those feelings had manifested in the form of back pain. Simoni believes muscular tension is caused by psycho-emotional problems and because he knew Coutinho well and what he was going through at the time, he didn't do a clinical exam, instead he spoke to Coutinho about what was taking place in his heart and mind, which is what Coutinho wanted to do. Simoni's holistic approach, his relationship with Coutinho and Coutinho's awareness of the problem and willingness to talk about it are all elements to a successful conclusion – Coutinho going back on the training field.

There are many players going through similar or more complex situations, but they consciously hide and unknowingly bury their feelings because they don't have a Simoni to speak to, or because things are more complicated.

Coping with challenges

Tap, tap, tap, tap, tap, tap… 'Now repeat after me…' Carey Mann is using two fingers to tap on various points around my body. Carey is an Emotional Freedom Technique (EFT) Practitioner. She contacted me online and offered to help me with an ankle problem I had developed from an injury nine months before.

I class myself as an open-minded person but while Carey is tapping my body and asking me to repeat different phrases I'm thinking, 'this isn't gonna happen'. She asks me to rate the pain in my ankle out of ten, rotates the ankle to assess and then she starts tapping away at the ends of my body's energy meridians. Gradually, I am absorbed into Carey's instructions, the tapping on specific areas, the repeating of affirmations and the brief conversations in between. Then she tells me to rotate my ankle one way and then the other. I look at her sideways. What has she done to me? My pain has dropped dramatically. I begin to laugh in shock! I giggle through the rest of the video, responding when I can as I find the shock overwhelming.

The video is on YouTube, so you can see for yourself. Just type in 'EFT clears stubborn football injury'. It is like watching a magician, but what did she do? Carey was counselling the trauma that I had been carrying from the injury that happened as result of an X-rated tackle, which I described earlier. My ankle felt different. It was the same ankle, but I had formed a different relationship with it. I no longer turned every tiny movement into a potential catastrophe. Players tear, snap and break parts of their body and only rebuild that physical part of the body, but what about the feelings that come with the tears, snaps and breaks?

I was never taught how to manage the issues I faced in my career, issues that were mentally challenging. I picked up a series of injuries that made me doubt whether I would make it from a training session unscathed, with every stride and every strike came a wince. I had to seek help from a professional outside football to help me trust my body again.

—**Danny Guthrie,**
former Liverpool and Newcastle player

Injuries are a big part of a player's career. A player may not just be out of action but can suffer psychologically too, becoming anxious about being in a vulnerable position. They also go from being engaged with and wanted, to being on an isolated schedule and, in some cases, ignored. With plenty of time to think and pay attention to the rumours, they begin to ask themselves, 'Will I ever play again? Will I be the same player? Are the rumours of the club buying my replacement true? My temporary replacement is doing well; will I get my position back? I have had a few injuries; will the club give me a new contract?'

The anxiety doesn't always stop when the player returns to action. The worry develops into a fear of the body breaking down, fear when sprinting or striking a ball after a hamstring or groin strain; the player is scared to turn around when in possession to make the pitch bigger after an injury. These fears are not always conscious, but an unconscious choice of preference, just like some players always using their preferred foot, even when it's less favourable to do so.

Players who have these fears often rule themselves out as injured. Some believe that their thoughts bring about the injury; others adapt their game leading observers to believe they have 'lost it'. Emotional injury is something that is rarely treated, and it results in players being dropped, sold or retiring, which brings a whole host of other problems.

I've had a lot of injuries and a lot of setbacks, starting with a ruptured ACL lateral meniscus tear and medial ligament damage. At that point, I heard people saying that my career was over or that my performances would not be as good. Not being in the team and only being spoken about in terms of my injury was hard. Being injured massively affected my mental state and self-doubt crept in. I began to question whether I would ever play again and if I were to play again, whether my performances would be as good. When I began to train again, it took a while for me to adjust to my body's changes as a result of the injury, find my confidence and get over my fear of breaking down.

I decided to ignore my doubts and began to look at my body objectively, as if it were detached from me. I studied its weak parts, researched my injuries, began to strengthen my body and moved from rehab into prehab. I carried out mindfulness exercises like meditative breathing and visualisation. I changed the fuel I put into my body and began to eat clean.

Football doesn't teach players how to handle these situations, leaving them in a place that affects their wellbeing. My previous clubs didn't have anyone we could see to get help when we felt down, at Manchester

City we have a sports psychiatrist the players go to see when they have problems. I don't see him personally, but the lads find him very helpful.

At the time of writing this, my body has sustained another injury just as I was working my way back to full fitness. I was feeling down yesterday, but I feel better now. I feel that my new lifestyle is key to my state and my overall outlook on life, strengthening how I view things on the whole.

—Fabian Delph,
Manchester City and England international

Seeking help with football mental health problems is becoming the norm. Players have access to help if they feel they need to see someone, but what about when they are unaware about how they feel? What about the players who, like me, unconsciously carried trauma around, or like Fabian Delph, who had to wait until he was overloaded with self-doubt, or Danny Guthrie who developed detachment from his own body? Is there a need to educate before the problems arise? A type of prehab for emotional injuries?

I have always been a fan of the creative therapies; therapies that go deeper than awareness and wander around the walls players put up. A player may want help, but if they unconsciously put up walls when they feel vulnerable they will block themselves from the help. Creative therapies such as Clinical Hypnotherapy, Neuro-Linguistic Programming, Timeline Therapy and Emotional Freedom Techniques help players to open their minds and reach beyond conscious awareness. There are senior players that have been in the game 20 years, that's 20 years of being conditioned not to show any weaknesses, in addition to the years of pressure of being male and following alpha male rules. Creative therapies provide unconscious processes for unconscious problems.

A few days after my EFT session with Carey, she did a follow up session with me over Skype, where she took me through a timeline intervention. I went back to speak to a younger me, at a time in football where I felt low – low on energy and self-esteem. I froze the scene and started to counsel my younger self about what I was going through at the time. Although this wasn't directly connected with the injury, I got to deal with emotional bruises I had experienced during my career that I had been carrying with me over the years without knowing. Bruises that changed my attitude for the worse when Charlton told me that they were not going to renew my contract.

So what are we left with?

It's a Friday, the beginning of October 2017, 5:15am. Before getting ready to hit the gym, I do my usual phone check and see that I have received a message from a former player that reads:

Hi this is ******** Firstly, my apologies. It's late, but I'm laying here in a hostel as this is where my life has taken me. I learnt 12 years ago never be afraid to ask for help. Well I did that with certain organisations and I got nowhere so I'm putting my neck on the line again and I'm going through my phone book as life has dealt me more challenges. I'm asking for a little financial help just to stay here, and food. I'm sorry to cause any ill feeling but there are only two answers and I'm brave enough for both. Thanks for reading this and God bless you.

I exchanged messages with the former player and struggled to shrug it off. I spoke with the Professional Footballer's Association who were already aware of the situation and had tried to help the man but he had been relapsing into his problems. I felt powerless and uncomfortable to know that a married man with four kids was in this position.

This is just an example of the many stories that keep

Sporting Chance and the PFA's welfare services active. Although it's important that players have privacy, it's also important to make people aware of the many stories that do not make the press. Many people inside and outside the game are unaware of the state a number of players are in.

Understanding mental health helps players to manage self. Understanding creates knowledge and knowledge is empowerment. Five key areas for players to discuss or coaches to discuss with players to improve understanding are:

- Identifying your feelings (within a context)
- Understanding your feelings
- Managing your feelings
- Empathising with others
- Being accountable and repairing emotional damage

Because everyone is vulnerable to mental health problems, education about wellness, mental illness and mental health as a whole is vital. As the examples in this chapter have illustrated, prehab is vital; there's a consistent service post-illness, but a limited service beforehand. If players know how to enrich their psycho-emotional condition they will make better decisions. Decision-making is the most important skill on the pitch and the most important skill off it. Decisions are governed by your state, and your state has the ability to distort your reality in a positive or negative way, from the options available to how you assess the intentions of others. Education on mental health improves wellbeing, financial literacy, performance and more, because it affects how you feel and how you feel affects your decisions. Mental health is not mental illness; everyone needs to be educated to make change, especially those who work with young people. Staff control the climate, so their development is also paramount.

A lot of the things we have been discussing depend on strong leadership. In the next chapter we will look at how some of the great football managers have achieved incredible things by taking into consideration the emotional needs of their players. We will examine the specific codes of particular players and find out what happens when managers tap into these.

SIX

LEADERSHIP

International businessman and food expert Clarence Francis' philosophy of management is that you can buy a man's time, physical presence and a measured number of skilled muscular motions per hour or day. But you can't buy enthusiasm, initiative, loyalty or the devotion of hearts, minds and souls. You have to earn these things.

When you look at leadership across different sectors, it begins and ends with the same thing: people. Leadership happens in all kinds of relationships including those you have with your parents, teachers and sports coaches. Your feelings about the way they lead you will affect your performance in those different environments: your behaviour at home, your success in a particular subject and your performance in sport. The same is true in the workspace, whether you work in the corporate world or the football world. Leadership governs performance.

Every season, all the teams at the bottom of a league have similar budgets and players and the same goes for those at the top. Once you get past monetary resources, what remain are human resources. These are the most valuable because they can help a team stretch past financial constraints. Use human resources well and you can exceed expectations. Use them badly and you can stifle potential. That's why a team at the top of the league can lose to a team at the bottom, and why a manager with a team of underdogs can win the biggest honours. The use of human resources separates good leaders

from extraordinary ones. Understanding how you feel as a leader, how those you lead feel, which responses to apply and the right time to apply them is highly demanding. It calls on skills that leaders across football traditionally have not been trained to use – relationship skills.

One of those skills is emotional literacy. The level of someone's emotional literacy will dictate how they direct a relationship and improve the quality of life of those they connect with. Emotional literacy involves:

- understanding your own feelings
- listening to others
- empathising with others
- repairing emotional damage
- expressing your feelings productively

If our spouse behaves in a particular way we feel loved, if a friend behaves in a particular way we feel disrespected and if a manager behaves in a particular way we feel motivated. We're all unique and have our own code, a way of responding emotionally to different stimuli. Something that makes one person happy and secure may make another angry and edgy. Know which buttons to press and you can trigger specific feelings in someone. If a leader makes us feel enthusiastic we will usually be motivated enough to do the task at hand.

Managing individuals

Good leadership is universal. A good leader should know how to trigger specific positive emotions in those they lead and be a role model in the management of themselves and others. Traditionally, football managers have behaved in the opposite way – hitting things and people, shouting and swearing. Yet players say that to be at their best they need emotional support from their manager above all else.

Human beings run mental processes that operate at a higher level than our thoughts, so we can guide and direct our actions, reactions and behaviours. These processes are the driving force behind our overall behaviour and determine our likes, dislikes, motivation strategies and more. Some people refer to these mental processes as meta programs, others refer them as our personality.

When people are all treated in the same way, it can create a feeling of fairness but may not be the best approach. People react to the same stimuli differently. In the football changing room, there are players who run different meta programmes and the managers more likely to get a positive response are those who understand this and use a variety of techniques and approaches to suit the individual they are dealing with. For example, when playing badly some players like to be shouted at, some like to be spoken with and others like to be challenged. Knowing the preferences of those in the team and being flexible towards players is a crucial skill that any manager needs in order to achieve success.

Football isn't about managing players; it's about managing people.
—**Chris Powell**
former Charlton and Leicester City manager

During Soccerex 2017, former England international Andy Cole spoke of his time playing under Sir Alex Ferguson at Manchester United and Graeme Souness at Blackburn Rovers, and the differences he experienced between the approaches. He explained that during his last season at Blackburn, he didn't care about playing football any more because of the poor relationship he had with Souness. Cole liked the club and the fans and enjoyed playing with his teammates, but the relationship with his manager affected his relationship with football as a whole during that spell. Cole drew a comparison between his two former managers, saying that Souness tried to control him, and how much he hated this approach (because it was contrary to his code). Sir Alex Ferguson, on the other hand, appreciated the uniqueness of each of his players. He understood and respected his players' codes and that is a key reason why his players achieved great things for him.

Just as 'the customer is always right', so is the player. Before a player is signed, the manager must ask themselves if they are willing to spend the emotional currency needed to make the player tick. If the answer is no then it is better for both parties that the manager doesn't sign the player. If the answer is yes then the manager must be prepared to pay the emotional price required to meet their needs. Souness ignored Cole's needs, which led to him not getting the best out of the player which then affected the team's performance and, as a consequence, his own performance as a manager.

What made Sir Alex Ferguson so special is he knew how to speak to each individual; he knew what to say to you in certain situations to get a reaction from you. Although he spoke to all of us, Sir Alex used to have a stronger connection with the senior players of the squad until Cristiano Ronaldo and Wayne Rooney arrived. He changed his approach and adapted his communication to engage the young players within the squad.

—**Quinton Fortune**
former Manchester United and South Africa international

Feeling important

Virtues and abilities are always better explored willingly. People perform the same task differently under the leadership of someone who treats them with disdain and someone who treats them with appreciation. As a manager, how you make your players feel and the way you tap into who they are is arguably more important than tactics.

Jose Mourinho appreciates the complexity of human beings and believes that knowing how to lead men with different childhoods, backgrounds and abilities is the most important thing when it comes to management. He acknowledges the value of emotional currency and taps into the psycho-emotional elements of his players to gain an advantage over his rivals.

In the chapter on unconscious competence, we saw that part of the game is played on autopilot. In the chapter on state, we learnt that a player's feelings govern their performance. If a manager can positively affect the state and the unconscious mind of his players then he will form strong bonds with them on a deep level that extends beyond the pitch, providing support and a nutritious foundation in which performances and wellbeing can flourish. As Alexis Nicholas mentioned, when Mourinho first went to Chelsea he made him feel wanted because he learnt about Alexis the person. Mourinho is known for investing millions in transfers and buying top players; he is also known for investing heavily in emotional transactions, getting to know his players as people and responding to their uniqueness.

Football has a lot to learn from other sports in terms of how to manage people. When we were at Chelsea, Mourinho was massive on the Neuro-Linguistic Programming approach to understanding players, so we all followed. I decided to do a NLP course and Alex Inglethorpe (Liverpool Academy Director) has just finished one too. Having an understanding of how players think, what motivates them and an interest in their wellbeing is key, it's not an addition to coaching, it is coaching. You're dealing with someone's son, when I became a parent I became a better coach, as I became more mindful of how I managed the person over the player.

I make sure I take time to have meaningful conversations with players to get an understanding of how their life is going. If you have a conversation with someone and it lasts five minutes they will tell you what you want to hear; if it lasts over 15 minutes you get to the crux of the story. For example, if I ask a player if he is alright, he will say 'yeah', but 15 minutes into the conversation they're telling me that they've had a row with their brother etc. I purposely set out to have conversations with them over set periods, organic conversations where I spend 70 per cent of it listening to the player. I can't do this with all the players, so I build bonds with about eight players from the 20 and the other coaches will have a stronger bond with another set, so all the information from the 20 comes back to the staff.

Coaches have the ability to create a life-long impact on a player. An example of this is a story that Benni McCarthy shared with me of his time with Mourinho at FC Porto. Mourinho told him to ring his mum, so he did. Mourinho took the phone and said, 'I'm going to make him a top player and don't worry I'll look after him.' Benni thought, 'Wow, I'm just a street kid from South Africa and this guy cares for me. I would've killed for him, no one has ever been like that with me.' All because Mourinho took the time to speak to his mother.

Feeling important is a feeling we all enjoy. There's a picture of Jurgen Klopp, Alex Inglethorpe, Pepin Lijnders and me on the balcony at the Liverpool academy on one of Klopp's first days at the club. That was the first time I met him. Klopp, who was one of the most wanted men across Europe, shouted, 'Hey Michael, are you still alive?' as I was walking up the stairs. I was thinking, 'What's he talking about?' like we've previously met. Then I realised that he watched Liverpool TV where I do a Come Dine with Me event, when our young players move out of their digs and into their own place. Klopp knowing about me and making a joke made me more relaxed and a positive way to start our relationship.

Hearing the impact Mourinho had on Benni, and being a parent, led me towards a mindful way of coaching. Klopp making me feel relaxed meant I now see the game differently and I regularly do professional development courses from NLP to Life Coaching, applying new skills to the elite players I work with. This is why Carlo Ancellotti is my favourite. I enjoyed working with him at Chelsea and being part of a project where the person is central to everything and the more I learn, the more I appreciate his resilience to stand by his style.

—**Michael Beale**
former Sao Paolo Assistant Manager and Chelsea youth coach,
Liverpool FC Head of Coaching for the Foundation Phase

Zlatan Ibrahimovic is known as the player that wears his pride on his sleeve. His famous quotes have been doing the rounds on the internet for years. He refers to himself as a lion, king of the jungle, and speaks about himself in third person. If you want Ibrahimovic to put more effort into his performance, then you must challenge one of the things he values most – his pride. He was going to receive an award for being the best foreigner in Serie A, so during a half time team talk when he was not performing at his best, Mourinho tapped into Ibrahimovic's code by challenging his pride. He told him that he might as well give the award to his mother, someone who actually deserved it. Needless to say, Ibrahimovic went into the second half fired up, promising to run until he tasted blood.

Playing into a player's self-concept is something Mourinho does smoothly and effectively, programming them towards the task at hand. A manager that can ignite that power in his players is a manager that has the power to make a difference, and a very big one at that. People are motivated by different things: some like to help others, some want money, some want status. Tapping into that motivational strategy will help players to give more than they consciously think they are capable of giving. Remember the example at the beginning of the State chapter where the mention of a hungry lion changed your feelings? That was because the lion triggered a specific response in you, a feeling of fear. The fear gave you a burst of energy and sensory acuteness that was consciously unavailable at the time. This is referred to as 'fight or flight', a physiological response when survival is threatened. Knowing how to trigger this is a great tool to have in your tool kit.

When it came to man management, Jose Mourinho and Tony Mowbray were the best. In a strange way they knew how to balance taking care of you and intimidating you. Mourinho had the money so he had to manage world stars; Mowbray had a limited budget, so he managed young stars. Mourinho was about rules; no one was allowed to go out. He had a code of ethics and at the front of the booklet was his number in case there were any problems or if you were unsure of anything. You had no excuse to step out of bounds.

I remember having a terrible training session with the first team at Chelsea. When the session ended I trudged off the pitch feeling sorry for myself and I felt this arm go across my shoulders and a voice say, 'You joined here at 21.'

Mourinho started to go into my history; he knew my strengths, weaknesses, everything. At that moment I wasn't feeling too great because I was used to Claudio Ranieri's regime: if you trained badly as a young player you would get demoted instantly and somebody else took your place. This had me on edge a little and was why I felt uncomfortable after a poor performance in training once Mourinho was the manager. He reassured me almost instantly by saying about a player's bad times, 'Fans remember those, coaches don't.' He made me feel safe. Other coaches I've had don't do this; they will tell you you're low on confidence instead of giving you confidence.

Tony Mowbray managed players very well, so well that they stuck to his word and followed his rules. I played under Mowbray at Hibernian FC. There were times when he would say that we shouldn't go out if there was pressure on us at that time. At other times, like after we got whipped by Hearts in our big derby match, he said that we seemed stressed and that we should go out. There was a balance which centred on the players' wellbeing, so we respected it.

—Craig Rocastle
former Chelsea and Grenada international

What motivates one can demotivate another. Listening to players and paying attention to their patterns will reveal their motivation strategy. For Benni McCarthy it was speaking to his mum. For Zlatan Ibrahimovic, it was tapping into his pride. For Wesley Sneijder, it was sending him on a holiday during the season because he looked exhausted. And guess what? Sneijder went on record to say he was ready to kill for Mourinho. Working with the individual motivational strategies of his players encouraged and motivated them, this is how Mourinho could work in different countries and achieve results. Because no matter where he went, he worked with the same raw material: people. So, he applied the same methods of human science to get the same results – trophies.

115 years of revolutionary men

The style of football we see played by Ajax, Barcelona, the Dutch national team, the Spanish national team and now at Manchester City FC, can be traced back to Manchester City 115 years ago and an Englishman called John 'Jack' Reynolds. Reynolds, a Mancunian, is known as one of the pioneers of Total Football, a style of play whereby outfield players can interchange while retaining the team's intended organisational structure.

Just like some of the most high-profile managers in the 21st century, Reynolds did not have a highly successful playing career. He started out at Manchester City FC in 1902 as a winger and clocked up most of his appearances (108) at New Brompton, now known as Gillingham FC, between 1908 and 1911.

After his playing career, Reynolds took the managerial role at St. Gallen's in Switzerland for two years before leaving to become manager of the German national team. However, the outbreak of the First World War meant he had to look for a role elsewhere. Reynolds ended up at Ajax, a club that had previously won nothing. This relationship between manager and club was the beginning of a revolution that would have an impact on the world of football for the next 100 or so years.

Managing Ajax intermittently for 24 years between 1915 and 1947, Reynolds laid the foundations of what would be known as Total Football in Holland and which evolved to Tiki Taka in Spain. He wanted his team to play with skill rather than physical power and so he implemented the same style of training, play and professionalism throughout the whole club from the first team to the youth teams, thus achieving success as one cohesive unit. Reynolds led Ajax to win the league eight times and the KNVB Cup, no mean feat for a club that had previously won nothing. In Reynolds' time at Ajax, he managed Rinus Michels and Jany Van Der Veen.

Van Der Veen, who went on to coach the Ajax youth team after his playing days were over, used the approach he learnt from Reynolds of working with mistakes, being creative in practice and having fun. Michels looked beyond the manipulation of the ball, extending Reynolds' tactics to the manipulation of space, using movement to make the pitch big in possession and small when not. Expanding the theory of Total Football, Michels built a philosophy around the style of play. This includes *maakbaarheid* (makeability), which involves the analysis, shaping and control of the environment. Michels' methods led Ajax to national and international honours, including three consecutive European cups.

Ajax now had a culture of winning in a unique way. As with any environment, when you bring someone up in a place that is culturally rich, the culture will become part of them. Bringing through players brought up on the principles of freedom, hard labour, a cognitively demanding ethos and strong philosophical beliefs creates a tribe. It was only a matter of time before the club birthed a talisman who embodied the Ajax way, and that talisman was Johan Cruyff. Growing up in an environment where Van Der Veen was his youth team coach, then Michels his first team manager,

Cruyff's transition through the club was a smooth one. In addition, Englishman Vic Buckingham also played a role in his transition, coaching Cruyff in both the youth team and first team.

Playing at Ajax, Barcelona and Holland, Cruyff and Michels were known as the biggest contributors and exponents of Total, and they took the Ajax model international. Although they had their differences, their professional relationship was the reason behind their success. Their long-term achievement was to create a culture whose high technical and tactical standards are still maintained to this day at three of the teams they both worked with: Ajax, Barcelona and the Dutch national team.

Just as Michels handed the baton to Cruyff, Cruyff passed it down to Pep Guardiola, a well-known mentee of his. Ajax and Barcelona still have a strong Total Football culture within their club, an example of this is Barcelona's La Masia, a football school that embodies the technical, tactical and emotional values of Total Football to create a 'total footballer'. Like Michels and Cruyff before him, Guardiola expanded on the style further, giving the world the best football that was being played at that time and, arguably, the best football ever. As well as introducing a new style of play, he offloaded some of the biggest names in world football, from Ronaldinho and Deco to Gianluca Zambrotta and Edmilson, replacing them with relatively unknown players like Pedro and Sergio Busquests. Guardiola showed that he was only going to approach the job one way – his way. After Barcelona he did a brief management stint at Bayen Munich FC before taking the management role at Manchester City. Ironically, Guardiola became the manager of Man City 115 years after the person who laid the foundations for Total Football left as a player. Things had come full circle.

From Reynolds' foundational work to Michels'

development of the methodology, from Cruyff's activism on the art of football to Guardiola's revised style, what all these men have demonstrated is that football is more than just kicking a ball. They successfully implemented a new philosophy and stuck to it, distorting the pitch and defying the rigidity of static positions. The resulting victories all helped to preserve and enhance the art of football.

Collective intelligence

In 1987, Arrigo Sacchi became the manager of AC Milan. At the beginning of his reign, the Italian media cast doubt over his ability to manage one of the most talented teams in the world, because he himself had not played at the top level. In response to the Italian press, Sacchi stated that he didn't need to be a horse first to become a jockey. Sacchi went on to transform the way Milan played, and to this day the world continues to debate whether or not his Milan team were the finest football team that ever existed.

When a new manager takes up their role they assess the squad, but the squad is also assessing three things about the coach: what they make them do, how they make them do it, and how they make them feel. If any of these three areas look doubtful then trouble is brewing. A manager with a good track record will be given a bit of time to prove the doubters wrong. But a manager whose track record doesn't match his players' ambitions has to act fast if the whole thing is not to prove a catastrophe.

The manager is the focal point. Once the manager passes the players' assessment, the squad will follow them whole-heartedly. Player assessments are often carried out unknowingly and relatively small things can make a big difference. When Mourinho shouted at one of his coaches in the early days of his first stint at Chelsea, Alexis Nicolas experienced a level of equality and unity that he had never known before and it created a positive impact. A group of people can be called a team, like a building can be called a home, but the quality of both is judged by how they make you feel.

Because of his unglamorous CV, Sacchi had already attracted extra attention. However, this was nothing compared to the extra attention he got because of his tactics. One of his core beliefs and selling points to his players was collective intelligence. His view was that football isn't born in the body but in the mind and so he targeted those he perceived to be intelligent players, emphasising that he wanted the many to become one physical unit with one intellectual strategy. Influenced by Cruyff, Sacchi's Milan played as one, sharing the responsibilities across the pitch, filling in various positions during the game with players continuously contributing to the fluidity of the performance, providing support in defence and assistance in attack, sharing the workload across the pitch. In deciding against having a team comprising solo artists, Sacchi created an orchestra.

Collective intelligence is a principle of mine. I know it sounds obvious but treating people with respect, being polite and giving others an opportunity to contribute to the plan and not just imposing what you think is the right answer is fundamental when leading a group. In my 20 years at KPMG in different management roles, this is something I've relied on and I've seen it become part of the culture of how we work.

—Tim Payne
Partner at KPMG (and In People Consulting)

Leadership discussions are often dominated by what the leader does. Sacchi provided a platform for his players to do more and this allowed his team to do great things. Leadership is about what leaders do; it's also about the environment they create, a place where they seemingly do nothing and their team does everything. Is it a coincidence that Sacchi, one of the greatest managers ever, and Tim Payne, quoted above and a partner for one of the biggest auditors in the world, both hold the same values? Giving clarity and a sense of value to team members, collective intelligence reaps the benefits that come from feeling as one and, as a result, raises the collective IQ of the group. Although collective IQ doesn't guarantee success, it does maximise the potential of the group. In a game based on decision-making, increasing the collective IQ makes the difference and, in the case of Ajax, Holland, Barcelona and AC Milan, makes them great.

Importance of interpersonal skills

The human voice is a medium we use to make friends, get a job and fall in love. It is also a medium we use to create conflict, damage relationships and to start wars. Man management or 'human science' is heavily driven by the communicative relationship. Yet despite playing an active role in our lives, our education on communication is limited to the refinement of the sounds that come out of our mouths and not the impact they have. It's no surprise that people unintentionally create negative feelings in others through the mismanagement of their words.

Sir Alex Ferguson was known for taking an interest in Manchester United's younger players and their families. Training ground interviews show him stopping himself mid-sentence to 'check-in' with others. Sir Alex Ferguson's efforts created what his former player Kieran Richardson called a 'family environment', which played a key role in the success of Manchester United during his time at the club.

In consulting roles, performance is more quantifiable in terms of client satisfaction, utilisation, winning projects and so on. In my experience of internal HR, it is less tangible. For this reason, I spent more time working with people on their careers – they were just less clear in the internal world. My success in this role couldn't always be measured by a number but dealing with emotions was an important part of the role.

I was told of a story a while ago of a senior banker that would go into a retail branch, greet everybody and ask them about their lives. He kept careful notes of these discussions and referred back to them the next time he visited. He showed genuine interest in the people working in his division. His behaviour increased productivity and staff morale, just by showing an interest in the lives of those he relied upon.

I'm a Manchester United fan and I remember hearing the stories about Eric Cantona staying behind to do extra training when everybody else had hopped into the showers. Needless to say, Cantona led by example, and that ethos seeped throughout the club. It's the same within the corporate world.

I was at a conference the other week and former Formula One world driver David Coulthard was one of the speakers. He was saying in Formula One when he was a racer, after every race the whole team would come together and discuss what went wrong, what could have gone better and how they could improve. These reflections took place even when he won, even when things went really well. After retirement he then went into TV production and after his first contract, he got the team together and said, 'Let's do a review.' People were saying, 'What are you talking about? We don't do that in TV, that's ridiculous.' He completely changed their way of thinking, he now has his own company and it's built on that kind of culture where you're always looking for an edge.

Finally, self-awareness in leadership and management is crucial, the ability to put themselves in the position of the person they're leading and managing and understanding the impact their words have on them. People work better when they are happy and feel that senior management consider their feelings.

—**Tim Payne**
Partner KPMG

Bravery is a trait that players are expected to have when playing in the professional game: bravery to tackle when they are not favourites to win the ball and bravery to take calculated risks with it. Bravery wasn't something players mentioned when they spoke about what they looked for or admired in a manager, however, lack of bravery was often the reason the manager upset them when avoiding a 'difficult conversation' for example, explaining why they were going to drop them. Bravery was often the reason they respected their managers, for example, when their manager had 'the difficult conversation' with them and was open, honest and transparent, regardless of the situation.

There are coaches who avoid conflict and players see right through it, which makes their job more difficult in the long run. They love the game, do their coaching badges to qualify as a football teacher, but remain ill prepared to manage confrontation, something that universally pops up as part of the role of a leader. Some coaches skilfully avoid conflict by delivering their message ambiguously. For example, 'Players need to start working harder otherwise they will be gone!' Who specifically? They have avoided naming individuals in order to avoid conflict. To be fair, it isn't always lack of bravery that is the cause. Some managers may deliver their message to a player indirectly if they think they might be feeling emotionally sensitive at the time or, in Tim Payne's case, they just feel tired at that particular time. But there are also those who avoid the conversation altogether. Once players see that their leader finds it difficult to lead them, they will find it difficult to follow the person's lead.

Stress levels are high in football. Managers dodging conversations that upset others cause more damage, as the conversation will take place one way or another anyway. Avoiding difficult conversations with players will have a knock-on effect on others and lead to the manager losing respect as a leader.

As social animals we are affected by our environment and we've looked at various types of environment in this chapter. Leaders are the people that govern the environment and can make an unhappy place feel better or a top-class facility feel like hell. Those feelings will then affect performance.

More than authority

It would take a great deal of research to understand the details behind Leicester City FC's historic season as Premier League winners in 2016, but what we do know is that the team was filled with players that the top clubs had rejected because they didn't think they were good enough. Something at Leicester clicked and allowed all their talent to flourish.

The manager of the Championship team was Claudio Ranieri. Apart from tactical and transfer decisions, Ranieri had to decide many other things on a micro level that affected Leicester on a major level. Things like how he would tell players he was dropping them, playing them in a different position, asking them to play while carrying an injury. Or, just as he did with Alexis Nicholas, asking players to step in when it is a high-pressured game.

When talking about management in football, results usually get the most attention. Some managers make the mistake of focusing on results while neglecting their players. The manager's role is to make sure everything is in place so that those in charge of getting the results are as prepared as they can possibly be. Leadership isn't about authority and results. The job gives you authority and the output of your input is results. Football managers who believe the role is about authority and results can 'lose the dressing room' quickly. More visionary managers understand it's about more than authority, results and even players. They know how to tap into a greater resource which governs performance – the person.

Michael Beale's work at Chelsea and Liverpool reflects the type of relationship he has with players and his coaching style. I met John Guehi, father of England Under-17 World Cup winner Marc Guehi, and when Beale's name came up in the conversation, John's face lit up. John spoke at twice his normal speed as he explained the positive impact Beale had had on his son. And on Liverpool:

Sao Paulo manager Rogerio Ceni came over to England to visit the Brazilian players at Liverpool FC. He went for dinner with Lucas Leiva, Roberto Firmino and Philippe Coutinho. He mentioned to them that he liked the Liverpool Under-23s coach (me). The players spoke highly of me and that's why Ceni decided to approach me to become his assistant manager at Sao Paulo. Ceni didn't tell me this story until I had been working for Sao Paolo for two months. He said that Lucas, Firmino and Countino all spoke about how I was with them on a personal level; they said my coaching was good, but my personal skills made the difference.

Alex Inglethorpe and I both see personal skills as part of the coaching package and not separate. It's something that I have had to work on as I'm shy. Whenever you hear the discussions about the best managers people often talk about 'man management', but what does that mean? When I take over a group, I put everyone's birthday in my calendar. Whenever I learn anything about them I try to remember it. If I don't remember that they have two boys and a little girl, I ask, 'how's the little 'uns?' or with the younger ones I say, 'How's mum and dad? Make sure you say hello from me.'

—**Michael Beale**
Liverpool FC Head of Coaching for the Foundation Phase

Beale's behaviour in storing his players' birthdays in his phone and interacting with them in his head is just like the senior banker I mentioned earlier who stored conversational data about his colleagues on his laptop. Both felt that it was important to listen and show an interest in the people they lead. Both have left lasting effects on people as a result of their approach.

Freedom to think

I coached Jack Wilshere at Arsenal when he was 14 years old, but I can't take any credit for the player that he is. I never say this about players, but at 14 I knew he was going to be a superstar. He was too good, so good that I used to play him centre back, right back and play him right wing. I would never play him centre midfield because he would get the ball from our keeper, run past everyone and score which meant he wouldn't develop and neither would his teammates. So I played him in different positions to create different challenges and develop his understanding of the game, so he could learn what the game looked like from various angles. I told Jack and his parents what I was doing and why, and they were OK with it.

—Paul Mortimer
former Charlton player and Arsenal youth coach

Working from the neck down is traditional football practice and what I refer to as 'zombie training', creating players that don't innovate within the moment, playing as though they do not have a brain. Paul Mortimer moved Jack Wilshere into different positions, he also moved Jack into his head. Playing out of the comfort of his usual position presented different problems; different types of players forced him to think of different solutions.

Instruction can work but is not as powerful as experiential learning. Experiential learning allows the player to go through the process, seeing and feeling the situation in detail. Talking to players about developing their decisions is one thing, helping them to go into their head to actively start the process is another. Paul helped Jack to do this as an advanced student, where coaches in other instances may leave the advanced student at the level they are. The same process can be applied at the other end of the scale when a player struggles to do the basics in their original position.

Telling players not to do something takes away freedom of expression. Creating activities that tells them not do something encourages them to express themselves in different ways. For example, if a player takes too many touches, instead of saying that, put a tackler on the player in training. The more touches the player takes, the more vulnerable they will be to a tough tackle. The problem will sort itself out.

What young players need

Speaking to the next generation of footballers from around the world I asked them, 'What do you need from your coach, so you can be at your best?'

I need a coach that knows when to be a little hard with me and knows when to be soft with me; once they know how to manage me they will get the best out of me.

—**Flo Van Den Eynden**
Inter Milan and Belgium international

I feel important when my coach takes the time to speak to me about my game and how I can improve.

—**Dusan Jajic**
Hammarby and Sweden international

I need my manager to support me no matter what, connect with me and give his all like he expects me to do.

—**Rijad Sadiku**
FK Sarajevo and Bosnia international

The confidence a coach can give you is unique. When I have my coach's time and attention, I feel valued which makes it easier to play.
—**Luca Ercolani**
Manchester United and Italy international

When I have a coach's support, he will get the best out of me.
—**Besard Sabovic**
Djurgardens IF and Sweden international

I need a personal relationship with my manager, someone that I can build trust with and always know that he is invested in me wholly.
—**Filip Djukic**
FC Copenhagen and Montenegro international

When my coach praises me, it gives me confidence.
—**Matthew Dennis**
Arsenal and England youth international

Directly and indirectly there's a strong need for support. Players are very aware that they are constantly being judged by everyone but one of the most important people they are judged by is their coach. He is the decision maker who decides whether they play and whether they get a contract. A coach can influence how a player feels about themselves and their performance, so their support is key, especially after a mistake. Players put their future in the hands of their coach, they make themselves vulnerable and because of this, players hope that their coach empathises with them, has compassion, is mindful and invests time into them.

When Graham Taylor took over at Aston Villa he had a real interest in young players. He would always come to our changing rooms, talk to us and just listen to our points of view; this gave me a huge lift!

We had a group of players that had just won the FA Youth Cup and a few in the age above that he was aiming to get into the first team. Taylor got me involved from the get go. At the time we had six senior strikers, he called a meeting with all the strikers and said, 'I wasn't expecting Stefan to be involved so soon but he will be involved'.

—**Stefan Moore**
former Aston Villa and England international

Players are confident that if they get the right support they can focus on football because they will be in the best place emotionally to do so. But without support they will not feel secure enough to perform to the best of their ability, opening them up to performance insecurity, stress, anxiety or depression. Players invest a lot into their careers, some moving across the world, leaving their families behind at a young age so support can affect whether they make it as a footballer and help maintain their psycho-emotional health.

Support is a generic word. Everybody seeks support in their own unique way from positive ad-libs while performing, to constructive criticism and praise of positives when going through a bad spell, personally or professionally. Whether it's grassroots football or professional football, football coaches for many youngsters may represent the only consistent figure in their lives they can attach to. The player–coach relationship often goes further emotionally than the professional limits and because of this, coaches hold great power over the development of players and people.

Aidy Boothroyd said we wouldn't shout at a kid when teaching them to read or write so why do we do it when teaching them how to kick a ball? We have to be mindful when speaking to players, especially the young players when teaching them.

—**Chris Powell**
former Charlton and Leicester City manager

From the beginning of the 2015/16 to the end of the 2017 I delivered 53 sessions to 24 clubs. The sessions were on emotional literacy with the focus being on player behaviour and how they treat others in their team. In three different clubs, players from different age groups shared that they felt unheard, mistreated and powerless at U13, U17 and U23 level. As a result, they said their performance levels dipped, causing more stress and creating a strain on the player–coach relationship and their life as a whole.

Creative education expert Sir Ken Robinson says great leaders are not like industrialists, focusing on logistics, command and control. They are more like farmers, because farmers acknowledge that they cannot make a plant grow, however, they are aware that the plant grows itself and that they can influence growth by the conditions they create. It is the same in every human system.

Football clubs are not machines although they operate in this way. They are more like organisms, organisms with players that blossom through feelings, motivations and aspirations. Like all organisms they flourish under certain conditions and stagnate under others. What top young players in the world are asking for, what Quinton Fortune shared, what Michael Beale practices and what Claudio Ranieri created were different stories about creating the right conditions.

> But what about the conditions that players have come from? Wages and a job help but they don't guarantee happiness or heal the trauma of growing up in a ghetto; they can't erase the effect of street culture. How can those responsible for their development and career help? That is the subject of the next chapter.

SEVEN

PLAYER PREMIUM

Craig Rocastle and I are at my mum's house, chilling in my bedroom. It's about 8:30 on a warm summer's evening and the window is open. Craig's sipping from his Lucozade bottle when suddenly there's angry shouting. I leap off the bed, knowing from long experience what the tone and commotion levels mean. 'Sounds like a fight ... outside my house!' Craig follows me along the corridor and down the stairs. The closer I get to the door, the louder the shouting becomes.

'What the f**k! Do you wanna die tonight?' my neighbour shouts at my mum's friend's son, who I'll call David. (My neighbour is a gang member and what I find out later is that he'd politely asked David to stop sitting on his fence, but David refused.)

'Do you want to die tonight, fam? You know what, wait there!' My neighbour storms into his house. Knowing that he is capable of anything, I'm doing my best to calm the situation while Craig watches on in bewilderment. By now David realises that he has messed with the wrong person but it's too late to backtrack, so he bolts into my house. My neighbour reappears at his front door, this time with a fully charged gun. Disappointed not to find his victim he walks towards Craig, raises the gun to Craig's head and says, in a slightly calmer voice than before, 'What you saying? Huh?'

Craig doesn't speak, so my neighbour repeats his question. At this point I intervene, tell my neighbour to go back into his house and, for the first time that evening, he listens to me.

I look back on that night in shock. Not so much shock at what happened but shock at how normal that scene had been to me as a young boy growing up. So normal in fact, that afterwards we just continued our lives as usual. The incident came up once in conversation but that was only because a few days after it happened I saw Craig talking to the guy who had put the gun to his head, and I asked him why he would speak to someone who had done that to him. (I believe that if someone disrespects you to that degree, you don't share your time with them.)

When he was 21, not long after this altercation with my neighbour, Craig signed for Chelsea FC.

Victims of circumstance

For teenagers growing up in Lewisham borough in the 90s, gangs, guns and drugs were commonplace, but to see a father present in any of our homes was strange. From the ages of six to 18, only three of my friends had both parents at home – and I had a lot of friends. Two of those three fathers beat the mothers and I actually saw it happen on one occasion when I was seven. Absent parents, overworked parents, lack of intimacy and an overload of aggression was the culture.

The lack of a secure person to rely on and make you feel safe, the absence of a loving environment, the sheer agony of not having enough money for meals can play out in destructive ways. I grew up with and worked with young people and adults alike who were killed, killed others, sold drugs, robbed people and went to prison for those very reasons. Here are the main themes I have noticed in people growing up in unfortunate circumstances.

- Using their lifestyle as an education to be mindful of others: These people demonstrate a high degree of care for others, some even using their old lifestyle as the motivation for their career choices. Former gang members, drug addicts and those who have grown up in that culture become mentors, teachers, teaching assistants, youth workers or take on roles where they can support others. Former Charlton striker Kevin Lisbie mentors young people and always speaks about the opportunities he got through football and how lack of opportunity negatively affected those he grew up with in pre-gentrified Hackney.

- Doing whatever it takes to fill their emotional gaps:
  This theme is characterized by misbehaviour. Misbehaving at school attracts attention from staff and from parents when they are asked to come into school. It doesn't matter that it's negative attention, just being noticed is what they have been craving all along.
- Becoming a victim to the lifestyle and behaving negatively as a result:
  Being shouted at and beaten by parents and people in the local area teaches some kids that this is what the world is like and that responding with anger and violence is normal. The displaced anger comes out in different ways. In an effort not be a victim some end up creating victims instead, building a reputation as someone not to be messed with. For others it plays out less obviously. They may find it hard to express a differing opinion calmly, they may not allow people to love them, they may not be comfortable with kindness or compliments.

When I was about 15 years old I intercepted the ball aggressively in a very difficult one-on-one situation on the pitch. Everyone was so impressed. I had no idea that I could use my aggression to be successful in football. Since that day I have channelled my aggression through my performances on the pitch to achieve success, express myself and feel good.

—**Gokhan Inler**
former Lazio and Switzerland international

Pupil premium

The Pupil Premium Fund is given to schools to help support any student who is eligible for free school meals, is in care or who has a parent in the armed forces. Every school gets a different amount, as the fund is dependent on the number of students who fall into the quota that year. For the schools I have worked in, the average has been between £250,000 and £300,000 per year; it supports those who struggle to fulfil their potential and have behavioural problems. Every school is required to disclose on their website how they spend their money and if you look at their sites you will see that money has been spent on personalised support, for example, identifying special educational needs or helping those who have English as a second language. From bringing in people to work specifically with individuals to creating an alternative curriculum, the search to make change is exhaustive.

Pupil Premium isn't about gangs or street culture but it does cover those who are at risk of joining gangs and acknowledges the street culture they are immersed in, something that plays a key role in professional sport. Street culture creates the players you admire, affecting their behaviour and the game in positive and negative ways. If there were a 'Player Premium' fund at clubs, there would be fewer stories of wasted talent and more success for everyone.

The value of the street

Street football is not about playing football in the street, it's about street culture. The sheer unprofessionalism of street football – the uneven surfaces, the unorthodox balls, the mixture of ages, the 20-a-side matches and the hours of conditioning – is what creates the culture. The uneven surfaces and unorthodox balls improve your touch and awareness of others in an environment that could have double the number of players of an official match. Playing against people years older than you brings intense physical and mental challenges because your opponents are more developed physically and have more experience.

The physical elements are important but there's something else in the 'street baller'; there's a confidence that comes through having faced every type of opponent in tough conditions. Being free to try things out, to make mistakes and learn from them in an adult-free zone builds the self-belief and resilience needed to maintain street cred. For some, street culture is not just about life on the gravel, it's about life off the streets too. All of these factors give players the kind of 'conditioning' situation that simply isn't found anywhere else.

When street players enter the professional environment, some are too raw and struggle to adapt. But some are a coach's dream; they have skills and personality, things that can't be taught, but can be refined.

Inter Milan had a deliberate uneven pitch for players to improve their concentration as the ball approached their foot.

—Michael Turner
Sunderland defender and Inter Milan loanee

I had friends that robbed banks, petrol stations and homes only to spend money on clothes. They would risk their dreams, freedom and life to impress others, gain acceptance into the street family and get control and attention.

Growing up in Lewisham borough during the 90s there were two gangs that dominated the area: Ghetto Boys and Brockley Boys. The Ghetto Boys were boys and young men from Lewisham borough. The Brockley Boys were boys from Brockley, an area in Lewisham borough. The two gangs patrolled the borough like siblings, with football being one of their mutual loves. During the summer holidays at Crofton

Park school there were 11-versus-11 matches consisting of Brockley Boys, Ghetto Boys and the sprinkling of others like myself who weren't in either gang. Some of those players either were in an academy at the time or went on to join academies.

The transition from being a Brockley Boy and wanting to hang out on the street to really taking football seriously was tough. When I was young although I never missed training, I would be up in the block (flats) up to no good. In those days fights, drugs, stabbings even murder were part of the Brockley life. Even when I was at Manchester City FC, I would go home every weekend and chill with my friends, I didn't do everything they did, and I had good friends too that would encourage me to focus on football, but I was around it. You can't make it and then just disappear even though one of the reasons I wanted to make it was to get away, like everyone does. It's tough but the culture was part of my life, the people were the ones I related to the most. The fact that my dad (Ian Wright) and my brother (Shaun Wright-Phillips) were both playing was an extra push for me. If I didn't have those two examples in my life I'd probably still be thinking I'm a thug and would still be on the corner.

Until the age of 27 a lot of things came before football. It's only in the last five years that I've had to put my head down as I wasn't where I wanted to be in my football career. I think the difference between the Bradley Wright-Phillips that played in England and the record-breaking Bradley Wright-Phillips of the New York Red Bulls in the USA is that although my dad and my brother played a key role in supporting my career, there was always the shadow of being Ian Wright's son and Shaun Wright-Phillip's brother hanging over me. I found it refreshing coming out here and starting again.

—**Bradley Wright-Phillips**
New York Red Bulls and England international

Times are different nowadays and the top teams have psychologists to help players with any problems they may have. But players must still be able to identify and understand their feelings and the 'abnormality' of their lifestyle before flagging them up as issues.

Timeline of an inner city London boy

There are players that carry a lot of emotional baggage from a young age. It's only now, as a 35-year-old adult, that I realise that many of my norms shouldn't have been normal at all, like my neighbour putting a gun to my friend Craig's head.

I grew up in the same area as Bradley: Brockley, south east London. To be a teenager in the 90s in our area meant you either were a victim of the gang or became a victim by joining one. There were many like myself, people not actually in the gang but close enough to know everyone in it and be vulnerable to the repercussions as an 'associate' member.

North, east and west London had similar issues with gangs and violence. Players would get together to talk about their areas, how 'active' they were and about the extremely talented players that should have made it as footballers but were lost to the streets. These were conversations being had by 14 to 16-year-olds.

To paint a thorough a picture I'll give you a timeline of my childhood and what I saw growing up.

Age 8: I saw the Ghetto Girls use their nails to rip the flesh off another girl's face at the Moonshot Community Centre. Moonshot was the hub for the Ghetto Boys.

Age 10: I joined the Moonshot football team, a team that has gone on to produce many for the professional game, the most recent being Arsenal's Reiss Nelson. There were Ghetto Boys in my team and they also surrounded the AstroTurf pitch we played on, like fans at a game. It was normal for someone to get a glass Lucozade bottle smashed over their head or be stabbed with the remains.

Age 13: People being robbed and beaten up was not news. I cannot remember the amount of times I'd stop people I knew from robbing others.

Age 14: Large numbers of my friends were selling drugs. People I knew began killing people and were being killed. Friends – too many to remember – were in and out of young offenders' prison and adult prison.

Age 15: I saw someone I knew on Crimewatch. People were excited and promoting it as though it was an achievement.

Age 16: The murders increased along with the prison sentences.

Other than my manager Kelly at Moonshot, I can't think of any coach I have played under who would have understood what I grew up around. Kelly had the respect of all because he genuinely had our best interests at heart and understood us.

My timeline is just a snippet of what I was exposed to and I wasn't an active gang member, they were just friends of mine. I was lucky enough to have a great family who gave me a strong foundation, helping me feel comfortable with myself and safe. Friends of mine who weren't so lucky struggle to this day to adjust to the professional space, be answerable to somebody else or follow another person's rules because doing so on the street would have made them extremely vulnerable.

From street culture to elite performer

Street culture spreads across sports and it's no secret that athletes from poverty-stricken backgrounds are some of the greatest talents the world has ever seen. Impoverished areas create a mix of unfortunate ingredients that benefit an athlete when competing. That's why football scouts purposely scour inner city estates looking for players with 'football character' – fearless, resilient, tough and ambitious. Being raised in an environment where they have seen and experienced things before their time creates a hunger in players to move their family away from those surroundings.

Richard Williams, father of Venus and Serena Williams, was determined to create tennis champions before the girls were born and mapped out a plan. After studying the sporting greats, he came to the conclusion that the best athletes came from the ghetto because it made them fighters. Leaving behind his wife Oracene and her three daughters from a previous marriage, Richard moved Venus and Serena into one of the most violent ghettos in the world – Compton which during the 80s was a warzone home to the Bloods and Crips gang where violence was a daily event.

He wanted to start training Venus by the age of five, but he had a battle on his hands. Williams' only access to a tennis court was through the drug dealer's headquarters and he didn't want needles, fights and murder so near to where he was going to train his daughters. Venus had already passed the age of five, but the gang showed no signs of leaving. A frustrated Williams took on the gang, physically fighting them over a two-year period, fights that would leave him with broken bones and missing teeth, unable to walk or breathe. This all took place in front of Venus and although he came off worst, she was inspired by his courage and determination.

Compton began to drain Williams physically and emotionally, but his flame was kept alight by the entrepreneurialism of others in their efforts to escape from their problems. The self-belief of two kids in particular stood out and inspired him. They sold records out of the back of their cars; they believed that they could rock the world. They went on to become Eazy-E and Snoop Doggy Dogg. Williams believed that if his daughters could make it in Compton they could make it anywhere. It was a huge risk to take, but the results have rewritten history.

Similar to the story of the Williams sisters is that of Mike Tyson, one of the greatest boxers to have ever lived. Tyson grew up in Brownsville, New York. Brownsville in the 70s was one of New York's most dangerous neighbourhoods. Getting bullied for being chubby and being referred to as 'little fairy boy' because his sister looked after him led to Tyson storing up a lot of unconscious anger and affected how he saw himself. His inner voice had the same tone as the bullies and his mother, who told him he was a piece of sh*t. This was why the future champion of the world didn't think much of himself and it caused his segue into gang life at an early age, committing burglaries from the age of eight, progressing onto full-time robberies that included robbing his teacher and using the money to buy clothes that he would wear to class the next day. The gang gave him what he was looking for: safety, love and acceptance. Tyson hated the feelings of being insecure, traumatised and afraid that came from being bullied in his youth, so he projected a ferocious image to the world.

Cus D'Amato, Tyson's boxing coach, took him under his wing and invested time and care in him, something Tyson was not used to. Cus changed how Tyson saw himself. His self-belief improved, he began to adhere to structure, set new structures, learnt to read, researched the history of boxing and worked out all hours of the day all in pursuit of his dream to become a boxer. Cus created a machine that was well-oiled physically, mentally and emotionally. The process of weaning Tyson off his old lifestyle was not a straightforward one. He committed the odd robbery, hiding out at Cus's house, which was some way from where he lived. Cus gave Tyson compliments, something that he yearned for from his mother but was repeatedly denied. He instilled limitless belief in the young man, gave him tutorials on emotional intelligence focusing on how to skilfully manage fear, and recommended that he research spiritual leaders. Cus became the person that Tyson was attached to, the one who made him feel safe and gave him purpose.

Cus passed away early on in Tyson's career and once he died, Tyson started going off the rails, visiting Brownsville more and taking drugs. By his own admission he didn't care about anything, he hardly trained for matches, fought just for the money and only wanted to party. Cus' death was Tyson's point of regression, returning him to a place of vulnerability, aggression and lack of attachment. He went back to square one, reliving the lifestyle of his younger years on the streets of Brownville. Tyson's mother and his surroundings led him to believe that he couldn't amount to much. His shame and fear lowered his self-esteem and made him defend himself aggressively.

Cus D'Amato played a key role in helping Tyson acknowledge his potential, fear and shame and use it to empower himself in the ring. The environment he created led Tyson to believe he could take on anyone and that is what he did, becoming the heavyweight champion of the world.

I came to England when I was seven without anyone, just me and my suitcase. I was coming here to stay with my brother but on the day that I landed in England my brother was sentenced to do five years in prison, so he rang someone while in prison to pick me up. I was a seven-year-old in a new country, living with a stranger. By the age of eight I was out on the street with 18-year-olds, doing dumb sh*t. I grew up too quick because I saw too much. Without going into the details, I was taking home £250 per week by the time I was nine years old. I got kicked out of school at 13; to me it was pointless me being there after the Year 11s from the year before had left because I couldn't relate to those of my own age. I never chilled with guys my age, never! At school I got into fights and other sorts of mischief and I just don't think the school knew what to do with me to be honest, it must have been difficult for them.

While this was going on I was playing for Millwall FC. I had been there from the age of eight and I loved it because they had older players that were from my area or that I knew from before like Marvin Elliott, Cherno Samba and Goma Lambu. No one knows this but when I got kicked out of school I became a full-time footballer at Millwall. As a 13-year-old I was loving it but everything changed when we got a new manager who wanted to separate the older players and the younger players and the divide caused disharmony. It was like we had two teams within one and that's when the fights began. Millwall during these times was crazy, knives were getting brought in, people were caught with guns at the training ground, the lot.

In the 2002/2003 season a lot happened. I played in every age group from the Under-15 team to the first team; nobody expected it. The things I was doing on the pitch were nothing different to what me and my boys were doing back on the streets of Wandsworth where I grew up. I was scoring consistently in all the age groups but getting increasingly frustrated which led to a number of small but significant incidents.

The straw that broke the camel's back was my fight with Mark McCammon, the striker whose place I had taken. Imagine the anger that builds up in a man who loses his place to a boy that is nearly half his age and gets constant banter from the team because of it. Just before Millwall's historic FA Cup final match against Manchester United FC, McCammon came in injured after playing a reserve game and the teasing started again with everyone asking him how he could let a 15-year-old take his place. Frustrated, he tried to deflect it back onto me by saying, 'Tell the truth, you're really 40 years old.' He was going on and *on but it didn't really bother me – I'd people bantering me about that for years back in Wandsworth. But then he brought my mum into it; that was a no-go zone. I told him to 'suck his mum' and then he punched me in the face. I was eating so I went for him with the knife and fork in my hand. Unfortunately, the papers' version of the story was that I went and got a knife and McCammon was lucky to be alive.*

Millwall tried to suspend me but there were complications due to my age – I'm not too sure of the rules around it. I was upset and angry, the papers ran their exaggerated story for two months and I had no family here to lean on for support. I was a young boy that had got up to mischief and had to face the consequences and rightly so, but no 15-year-old should be getting picked up by their neck or punched in the face by grown men. Sometimes I felt as though I was being punished for not allowing people to walk over me. I was going to defend my honour. From the age of seven I'd had no one to look out for me, so I had to look out for myself.

The impact of that incident affected the rest of my career. I had loads of clubs in a short space of time and although popping my anterior cruciate ligament played a part in that, the exaggerated story of my fight with Mark McCammon had everyone scared of me. I would shout at other players like all footballers do, except everyone would start to panic. It got to the stage where I would leave a club before they released me. It happened so many times that I was able to read the signs. Everywhere I went everyone kept bringing that knife story up, I was never able to shake it off.

Eventually, I left Millwall and went for a trial at Manchester City for three weeks of pre-season. I really enjoyed it there and was on trial with the likes of Kelvin Etuhu, Micah Richards and Daniel Sturridge. I was supposed to sign for Man City but ended up going to West Ham for the last week of pre-season and signing there, apparently West Ham United FC were offering more money. Leaving London would have been the best thing for me at the time. Ever since I was 15 at Millwall everyone had always treated me as a first team player which was great in terms of my progression, but they were also treating me like I was an adult when I was still a vulnerable young boy. I think my brother ruined the Man City deal; he'd taken over my affairs after he came out of prison. He wanted to be in charge of everything, but I felt that he was looking out for his own interests over mine, so we no longer talk. We even got into a fight in front of my biological mum on one of the rare occasions she came over.

When I signed for West Ham I was 16 and the first thing they did was send me on loan to Gillingham. Bearing in mind my background and history that was not the best thing to do. To make matters worse even though I was a striker who had scored goals for all the Millwall teams and for England, manager Neale Cooper played me on the wing. During my last game for Gillingham, I got sent off. Neale said it was pointless extending my loan as there were only six games left and I would be banned for three of them. I told him 'I'm not a winger, I'm a striker. I would have scored more goals for you if you'd played me as a striker, you've wasted my time here.' He didn't like my comment but as he was responding a lady walked in with an England call-up letter for me. Neale didn't even know it was for me, in fact he knew nothing about me at all, yet I played for his first team. I took the England letter, which infuriated him even more, and off I was back to West Ham.

Scoring in every game for the reserves led to me being on the bench for the first team but because I had been on the bench at West Ham I ended up being on the bench for England. I was fuming. Then, out of the blue, West Ham released me. It was strange because I was a young England international that was scoring goals for fun. Rumour has it that the West Ham manager at the time Alan Pardew found out that I was driving without a licence so he wasn't too keen on me. I shouldn't have been doing that, but why didn't he, or anybody else at the club, speak to me? I was just left to my own devices because they had already decided I was a bad boy. I could have done with support to help me make better decisions.

So, I set off for Glasgow Rangers. Alex McLeish signed me; I liked him and he was good with me. I loved it at Rangers. Because the Scottish Premier League teams had to have three outfield players under 21 in *their match day squad of 18, I was always on the bench because I knew that there was no one better than me in the Under-21s. Every game it was Charlie Adams, Ross McCormack and me on the bench. The young players at Rangers were good and we taught each other a lot. I learnt how to ping a ball at Rangers, something I hadn't learnt at Millwall, where it was kick, run and shoot. The day I signed my contract at Rangers, Neale Cooper walked into the club. He was there to see friends and I thought the timing was ironic as he'd told me I'd never make it.*

Eventually, Alex McLeish got sacked and went to Birmingham City. I was going to go with him, but Paul Le Guen came in and everyone told me to stay as Le Guen liked to play the kind of passing style of football that I liked. I signed the three-year deal that was on offer and bought a new Mercedes, cash. Pre-season came around and we did long-distance running for the first two days. I was great at short distance running and rubbish at long-distance running and no matter how hard I tried my terrible long-distance form continued and I ended up on the bench. My flat mate at the time, Charlie Adams, was playing and couldn't understand why I wasn't playing.

Then I was back in the reserves. Playing reserve football didn't bother me as I've never been big time, I just loved playing football and I scored every game.

Still young enough to play for the Under-19s I went with them to Germany for a tournament. This tournament had the world's best there: Real Madrid, Barcelona, Bayern Munich, everyone, but I got player of the tournament. As soon as we got back Bayern Munich and Barcelona phoned Rangers to express their interest in signing me. I was signed to Tony Finnigan's agency and he represented Aidy Boothroyd who was the Watford FC manager at the time, so I went there. I shouldn't have gone back to London, especially with Munich and Barcelona interested in me, but Watford tripled the wages that I was on at Rangers and I wasn't looking at the bigger picture.

It worked out for me when I first went to Watford, as I was playing in the first team but two months in, I snapped my leg in three places and was out for a year. I came back pre-season; we played Boreham Wood and won 3-1, with me scoring two of those goals. The next day I was told that I was going on loan to Swindon Town. I was being rushed back to full fitness. On loan I noticed that I couldn't manoeuvre properly (which I later found out was because one of the screws in my leg had come loose) so I went back to Watford to recover. I had agents, but I wish I'd had better advice and someone who could have stood up for me, I felt like I had no one to speak to. Malky Mackay replaced Boothroyd as the manager during this time and he offered to pay up the remainder of my contract, but this was after the transfer deadline, so it was difficult for me to find a club.

Just like when I was 13 years old and nobody knew that I was full-time at Millwall the same happened again, except this time I was 21 and going back to Millwall without the fans or the press finding out about it. I played a behind-closed-doors game against Portsmouth FC. We weren't sure how it would go down with the fans and deep down I didn't want it enough. Old injuries restricted my movement and led to new injuries.

Looking back at my career I see a boy that that had a lot of anger, I also see a boy that was scared. On the surface I looked confident and aggressive, but when I felt the most scared I showed the most aggression. My mum had taught me from a young age not to let anyone bully me, so if someone tried to bully me, either we would have to fight or they would have to leave me alone. Maybe people expected me as a 15-year-old to let first team players punch me in the face or lift me up by my neck but my mum's words and the methods of survival in Wandsworth taught me different. I was all I had. Everything I knew I had taught myself, every time I got into a problem, I dealt with it myself because that's all I had to rely on and was why I didn't listen to others.

I am lucky enough to have an adopted mum who still looks out for me to this day, but my biological parents are back in Nigeria. My dad passed away last year and people asked me if I was going to go his funeral but I didn't see why I should, as I didn't know him and he made no effort with me. Neither does my biological mum for that matter. One by one, the relationships with my family members have disintegrated. Some tried to place cultural expectations on me like calling people 'aunty' and so on. I thought 'Are these people for real? How can they expect a boy left to grow up on the streets to follow those traditions and call people I don't know or don't look out for me "aunty"?' I told them where to shove it! Another example was when I sent 10 iPods to family back in Nigeria. I was earning a lot of money, so it felt the right thing to do. I'm not a flashy person at all; to this day I don't know much about iPods, all I care about is the memory, so I can store loads of songs on it. Anyway, they sent the iPods back because they weren't the latest version.

I was a young kid being punished for my behaviour but not being educated or supported. I don't know how football is now, but I hope that there is more understanding and support for players who come from similar backgrounds to myself because I never felt that I had people I could relate to and really look out for me. Whether it was my family, club staff or my agents, to them I was just a commodity.

—**Moses Ashikodi**
former Millwall and England international

How their 'ghetto' plays out

The ghetto background will play out in different ways, from cultural preferences to how those from the ghetto respond to the world around them. Everyone is a product of their environment. Tyson's ghetto manifested itself as aggression, born from being bullied when young. Referring to himself, Zlatan Ibrahimovic says that you can take the boy out of the ghetto, but you can't take the ghetto out of the boy. Ibrahimovic was from Rosengard, a city district of Malmö, known as the most notorious ghetto in Sweden with police urging its citizens to help them bring down the crime rate. In his earlier years, Ibrahimovic was first a victim of his environment then a product of it, from getting his bike stolen when he was little to stealing bikes as he got older, including one belonging to the assistant manager at

Malmö. Ibrahimovic rode into training on stolen bikes while the parents of those he played with drove them in. His teammates passed their way through games; he dribbled his way through games. Everything about his home life and his time in Rosengard is reflected in his performances.

He used street football in Rosengard to practise the skills learnt from watching his Brazilian idols and describes his childhood as no hugs and no one checking in to see how you were feeling. This sums up his approach to football, from the artistic solo runs and acrobatic goals often associated with Brazilian players to his no-nonsense approach towards the game and his teammates, mirroring the lifestyle he grew up around. Proud of his ghetto roots, Ibrahimovic credits it with teaching him everything he knows about football which led to him winning trophies across the top clubs in Europe.

The gun and drug culture experienced by Watford FC's Brazilian forward Richarlison shows in the fearlessness of his approach. The £11.5 million signing from Fluminense, who has attracted interest from the biggest clubs in the Premier League, has said that he doesn't fear playing against the top teams because he had bullets flying past his face when he was younger, and a gun pointed at his face because a drug dealer thought he was trying to sell drugs in his territory. It's fair to say that Richarlison's fear threshold is far higher than the average person's.

I was lucky I had parents that were there for me when I was growing up, without my mum and dad I would have fallen victim to the streets because all my childhood friends are real street gangsters. I was born in Lea Bridge Road, Leyton, on one of the most notorious estates: Beaumont Estate. Truth is, my dad made me fear him more than I loved the street. I couldn't go check girls or go out on Beaumont Estate. My dad told me to be home by 4:00pm, if I wasn't home my dad would bust my arse! If I hadn't had that my life would have been lost to the street and I would never have made it as a footballer.

My dad went to work at 4:00am to do his first job as a postman then came home only to go straight out to do another job so he could get me to football. I remember once I was late and when I arrived my coach shouted, 'Who do you think you are?' I didn't expect him to know my story, but I was a kid, all he had to do was ask me. My family invested so much into my being there, my parents had me when they were young and were juggling a lot so that I could live a 'normal' life. It would make me, and others like me, very despondent at times.

As I got older and travelled to training by myself, I had to go across the city from east London into areas I wasn't supposed to be in – rival gang territory. Although I wasn't in a gang, I still had to have my wits about me. When I got into football there was a geezer that didn't understand what it had taken for me to get there screaming at me. 'Why is your face miserable? Why are you wearing that?' My coaches didn't understand what I was going through and I couldn't relate to any of them. When I tell the people in Brazil what I went through in England they can't believe it because the coaches are sensitive to the lifestyle the boys in Brazil are exposed to, how much it takes for them to get to where they are and how it affects them on the whole. The players come to training with lines in their hair, they dye their hair all different colours, but it doesn't matter, the coaches are not trying to change them, they are just trying to educate them tactically. On the pitch they don't tell them not to use skills, they give them advice on the most effective spaces to use those skills. Whereas when I played in the professional academy system in England, if we controlled the ball with the outside of the boot or in an unorthodox way, a natural way some of us learnt from our time playing in the park or in the streets, we would be shouted at and told to control the ball in a particular way. Everyone had to play in this way, even if it was unnatural to a few. The change was forced and not taught, needed or not.

This is where a player loses his identity. He is expected to know who he is, but he doesn't. That's when people begin to say, 'He used to be good'. He is still good, the talent is still in there but now it's locked up and pushed aside as self-doubt dominates his natural instincts. When I was on the come up, coaches were not coaching me and trying to develop what I had and what they admired when first seeing me play on Ive Farm (Leyton). Instead they were trying to change my character and my natural reactions instead of cultivating, adapting and fine tuning them. Looking back, I think how strange it was. If I wasn't what they wanted, they could have picked from millions of other kids as I am sure one of them would have fitted their mould.

Understanding inner London youth culture, what the players are going through, knowing how to speak to them, will affect their football in one way or another. If a coach has no understanding it will have a negative effect and if they do have an understanding they will have a positive effect.

—**Colin Kazim-Richards**
Corinthians and Turkey international

Street culture: 'character' building?

The stories of footballers in this chapter give some insight into the environment they grew up in and the type of network they have access to. Although the examples are of players that escaped the gang life, many fall victim to street life before they are able to make a name for themselves.

Former Liverpool and then Tranmere Rovers keeper Michael Kinsella was not as fortunate as the others mentioned here in terms of a football career, but he has used his experience to achieve success in another field. Kinsella entered gang life shortly after being released by Tranmere when he was 20 and began to sell cocaine. Former neighbours, classmates, players and kids in the local area often form the network to the underground, whether players want access to it or not. Sometimes players distance themselves from those types of old friends, sometimes they stay in contact with them and, as in Kinsella's case, sometimes they re-engage. Kinsella joined an international drug gang because he had access to the network via his social circle and needed money. Players that fall out of football while young can go and get a job like anyone else; however, they have been exposed to a potentially high-earning lifestyle within a few years of leaving school and when that opportunity is taken away from them they believe that turning to the streets is the only way to achieve that lifestyle. It was reported that when police raided Kinsella's home they found a contact list of drug dealers, £300,000 of cocaine and that Kinsella was one of the main men in the gang clocking up a £1.6 million fortune. He was sentenced to nine years in prison. With the gang life behind him Kinsella set up O.N.S.I.D.E, a company that supports those released by professional teams to prevent them falling to the trap he fell victim to.

With no support, and with easy access to people who appear to be living the lifestyle of a player through gang activities, it becomes an easy option for some to take. In March 2017 I was delivering an emotional literacy programme to Wandsworth prison inmates, only to have former Premier League player for Charlton and Fulham Nathan Ashton walk into my class. Nathan had six years remaining on a sentence for armed robbery. Like Kinsella and other former players that fall victim to the streets, Ashton struggled to adjust to the lifestyle that came with no longer being a player.

People like Inler, Wright-Phillips, Ashikodi, Ibrahimovic, Richarlison and Kazim-Richards are the reason why football clubs target players from the streets, building satellite centres within at-risk areas in order to get first pick of the players who possess the kind of character everyone wants in their team. Socio-economic problems channelled into motivation, social intensity syndrome (SIS), lack of emphasis on emotion, high risk activities and defending your honour all play out on the field as 'football character' demonstrated by fearlessness, aggression, hypervisualisation and responsiveness.

Football clubs talk up the benefits of street culture, but they come at a cost that will at times require extra attention and care. There is no set formula because every player is unique and so is their story. Some stories can be easy to identify and understand while others can be confusing. For example, Bradley Wright-Phillips had a career at the top but was very much involved with his old circle of friends and their destructive behaviours. Confused, fans and club staff may wonder why he did this when he had so much to lose. What is there to miss about the lifestyle of his past? He had the dream job, the money, everything. So why risk it? To the player it isn't seen as a risk, it is seen as being around people that treat him like a human being, it is seen as going home, it is the arousal deficit that leaves him craving social intensity. Social Intensity Syndrome (SIS) happens when people go to war. A lot of kids in England are at war throughout their childhood; war on the streets or on the pitch can both create the euphoria of being part of a high-intensity group. Someone with SIS can't be expected to embrace the comedown after a match or training; they thrive on intensity of emotion. For this reason, clubs must consider the emotional cost as well as the financial cost when they sign a player with a challenging past. If a club sees signing the player as giving them a lifeline then there's a strong chance the player's time at the club will not be a success. You only have to look at those 'bad boy' players who bounce from club to club or those who do not make it far enough to have their names known. If a club chooses to enter into a relationship with a player, then they must acknowledge the commitment at hand. They must acknowledge the player's problems and agree to work with them, because the way the player has handled themselves in the past is proof that they cannot do it alone. This is where Cus D'Amato set the blueprint.

Poor inner city ghettos create the richest of talents. Venus and Serena Williams were tactically brought up in their environment. They had both parents available, didn't have to worry about their basic needs being met and led a consistent, structured lifestyle. Ashikodi and Tyson, on the other hand, were victims of their environment. But playing in the Premier League and being an international footballer or being champion of the world and having a $400 million fortune did not make up for what was missing within them. Street culture powered their careers, however, attachment was fundamental to the outcome of their careers, and neither lasted as long at the top as expected. Venus and Serena had the consistency of two parents at home that provided structure, guidance, safety and support. Moses didn't have any attachment while Tyson had it briefly in the form of Cus. The three stories show the importance of attachment in general and Tyson's story alone highlights the power a coach holds, taking someone from young offenders' prison to world champion because he tapped into who he was at the core.

Steps to change

Growing up in difficult conditions leads to emotional infertility and non-ideal ways of behaving. The welfare of the person governs the player: if the person is fine when they play, their performance will flourish, not the other way around. If a club invests in its people, they will get better players.

Here are steps towards positive change when signing vulnerable players:

1. **What the player brings into the environment (dispositional qualities):**
   Think about who the player is, their upbringing, the environment they live in and their traits.
2. **What the environment brings out of them:**
   - How does being in a professional environment affect their behaviour?
   - How do they behave towards authority and rules?
   - How does the professional environment contrast with the environment they are from?
   - Who is the authority in their environment and how do they treat them?
   - What types of rules or social laws must they adhere to in their environment?
   - Do staff behave like or remind the player of a negative person in their life?
3. **What their behaviour brings out in staff:**
   - How do the staff behave towards the player that 'misbehaves'?
   - Are they aware of the background of the player and what the environment brings out of them?
   - Does the player behave like or remind the staff member of a negative person in their life?
4. **Assessment of the relationship:**
   Assess the behavioural cycle of points 1, 2 and 3.
5. **A player-led plan:**
   Create a plan (with alternatives), then ask the player to create a support plan detailing how they would like to be supported. The reason for creating a plan first is because some people do not know how they would like to be supported so your plan can provide some suggestions.

6. **Execution:**
   All staff that come into contact with the player must embrace and be committed to the plan.

Whether it's an academy or a first team club which sells and releases groups of players every year, each player represents a blank cheque whose value is based on how they play. How they play depends on how they feel. The club and the coaches can influence that a great deal if they approach the situation sensitively and with awareness.

> In the end, it's about relationships. Players have intense relationships with teammates, management, agents, family, money and with the game of football as a whole. Some struggle to manage these relationships because of their background, as we have seen, but also because of lack of education, emotional instability or the behaviour of others. The resulting mismanagement affects the behaviour of all involved and can have a lasting effect. In the next chapter I will delve into the different types of relationship, the health of those relationships and give tips for positive change.

EIGHT

FOOTBALL RELATIONSHIPS

Your football IQ is the most valuable thing you have.
—**Josh Sargent**
Werder Bremen and USA International

When I was growing up in the game, I would hear a lot about former Arsenal player David Bentley, who is two years younger than me. I remember the first time I saw him play: my Charlton Under-19 team had performed badly on a Saturday morning against Southampton FC so we had to train the next day, a snowy Sunday, while our Under-16s were playing against Arsenal. I didn't understand how we could learn anything by coming in on our day off to run in the snow after our defeat, so I was fuming! After we'd finished our running, my teammates and I had to walk past the Under16's match on our way to the changing room. My mood changed once I saw an Arsenal striker pull away from the goal towards the halfway line, receive the ball on the half turn and smash it against the cross bar from 30 yards out. This was before football clubs stopped the public from entering the training grounds to watch academy games. I remember turning to ask the audience, 'Who is that?' There was a mumbled chorus of, 'Bentley, David Bentley, Bentley, Bentley.' Everybody knew who he was, and it wasn't long before the world did too. After bursting onto the scene for the Arsenal first team and scoring an audacious chip against

Middlesbrough, Bentley went on to play for Blackburn Rovers FC, Tottenham Hotspur FC and more, but eventually walked away from football when he still had many years left in him. Why?

Also known as the next Dennis Bergkamp because of technical similarities to the Arsenal legend, Bentley fell in love with the game watching the likes of Paul Gascoigne, Eric Cantona, Benito Carbone and Georgi Kinkladze. Wanting to follow in the footsteps of his role models, Bentley would try to recreate their skills only to be accused of not taking football seriously. Sticking to his guns, Bentley continued to play the game the way he believed it should be played: with creative freedom. Before retirement, his frustrations increased along with the increased role data played within the game. The importance placed on how many times you ran and how fast contrasted with how Bentley believed the game should be played and his enjoyment of it began to decline. Not wanting to play the game for money, a disillusioned Bentley walked away from football.

Data is neither good or bad for football. I like data as I am someone who likes to work from facts, however, I know players who don't like data as they believe it's not reflective of the reality of the game. Data tells you who is doing what they should do and who isn't doing what they should do. You can be running 50 kilometres per game and not be a good player, or you can be Lionel Messi, getting 60 goals a season and not running as much. 15 years ago, a smaller team were more likely to lose against the top four teams in the Premier League because they were not as professional and didn't have the talent to compete. Nowadays, the smaller teams may not have the talent to compete with the teams further up the league, but they have systems in place to give them the best opportunity possible with the resources they have, making them better physically, technically and mentally, improving the league as a whole. Teams are buying players because they can run more and make interceptions, so there's less technical talent in the game but more hard workers.

—**Gael Clichy**
former Arsenal and France international

The relationship players have with football is unique. The game allows players to connect with a part of themselves that can be difficult to access anywhere else. The pitch becomes the place where they can express themselves, using their performance to channel their feelings and escape from painful reality or using their skills to create an entertaining masterpiece. Until the late 90s, the passion was developed through love: love of playing outside the house with a stone, in the school playground with a tennis ball, in the football cage on the estate or in the local Sunday league team. Through hours of playing, a game you liked developed into a love affair and then became a passion. Players decided which teams were fair, argued about decisions, celebrated victories, laughed at each other's mistakes, got into fights, cried, and created loads of memories. Whether or not they played for their local team, they governed the environment and had the freedom to express themselves.

This relationship with football had youngsters bursting to go out and play, happily missing dinner to stay out longer. They committed themselves to a sport just for the love of it and fell in love with the game because they were allowed to. So, what's happened? The answer is that society has changed; there have been surveys showing a drop in the number of kids who play outside and in spaces available for kids to attend for free. Access to football comes at a cost. If parents can afford to send their child to a football training camp, there's less time to 'play', have free time with the sport, be curious, practise sequences and improvise with the ball. Becoming a professional footballer takes years of physical and emotional investment, which is willingly exchanged for the platform to be free, a platform in this context being the bridge of expression between the game and the player's heart. When there is no bridge and a lack of connection, players turn their backs on the game, or play for what they can get out of it rather than what they can contribute to it. There's an expectation that you should love the game, yet you aren't allowed to fall in love with the game.

Not the whole story

In a four-year cycle, the fox population in northern Canada goes from a high to near extinction, only to spike and eventually return to its original high. The cycle repeats itself continually and the story wouldn't give a biologist much to work with if they were to focus on the foxes alone, as there would be nothing to explain the variation in population. Open up the research to include the relationship of foxes to others, however, and you will see the bigger picture: in this case, the foxes' relationship with rabbits. The foxes survive by eating rabbits and the rabbits have no other enemy in the habitat yet, like the foxes, they get to the point of almost dying out only to have a spike and eventually return to their original maximum population numbers. Marrying the cycle of foxes and rabbits together reveals the same pattern in the opposite direction. When there are more foxes they kill and eat more rabbits, this reduces the rabbit population and means less food for the foxes. Less food for the foxes leads to an increase in fox deaths which gives rabbits more time for procreation and survival, so the rabbit population increases. This in turn provides more food for the remaining foxes so the fox population then spikes towards its original high and the cycle continues. My point is this: data can only tell you so much. It's a story, but not the whole story.

My time in scouting has stretched across clubs that include Millwall FC, Brighton Hove Albion FC, Liverpool FC and my current club Manchester United FC. Back in the day, data meant scribbling notes on the back of cigarette paper and analytics were the eyes and ears of the scout. Now computers have taken data and analytics to another level and I find them a great support when building a dossier on a player. Being able to see what a player can do with a ball is one thing, seeing how they affect the group and what their lifestyle is like is another. I document everything I hear and see on and off the pitch, assessing character, mentality, family, attitude and more, making sure that I recommend good people as well as good players.

—**Mark Anderson**
scout for Manchester United FC

The data being collated across football clubs records the physical outcomes and the results of those outcomes and includes victories, distance travelled and individual achievements. This kind of data plays a part in whether managers get a job, keep their job or are sacked, which players are signed, play or get released, and which tactics are applied or rejected. When used to support decision-making, data can be of great assistance. If it's used to lead decision-making it can be like the fox: it only provides part of the story. Data recordings don't measure feelings or decisions, the very things that govern performance and separate the bad from the good, and the good from the great. The extra bits of information, the 'rabbit' so to speak, may be hard to see or record but they can be felt. To measure the leadership of former Liverpool midfielder Steven Gerrard, the organisational skills of former Inter Milan defender Laurent Blanc or the intelligence of Andres Iniesta would be impossible. You can compare data of what happens when those players are in the team and when they are not in the team, for example, clean sheets, goals scored, possession and so on, but they are only the by-product of their soft skills or football IQ. Gerard Pique once said of his Barcelona and Spanish international teammate Andres Iniesta, that in the world of data no one would sign him because he doesn't score loads of goals or create loads of goals for an attacking midfielder, yet he will go down in history as one of the greatest attacking midfielders in world football.

The leadership skills of Steven Gerrard, Laurent Blanc and Andres Iniesta are obvious to football lovers. But when they are in the team, do they take something away from those they lead? It's here that observation skills are key. Did Gerrard's leadership, for example, stunt the leadership capabilities of others? When on international duty, if Gerrard was injured or on another team in training, did his centre midfield partner play a better game when out of Gerrard's shadow? Naturally, a hierarchy forms within groups and people take up different roles based on the requirements of the group, their skillset and how they value themselves in comparison to others. If you looked at the data for the kind of game we are talking about, Gerrard's fellow centre midfielder may have racked up the same numbers in terms of goals, assists, distance travelled and so on when Gerard was not playing and yet the team might have scored more goals as a whole because the centre midfielder was more daring. You see, data will record a forward pass but not the risk attached to it. Risk can't be recorded, but it's felt; risk can bring greater rewards. A player is more likely to take risks when they feel they are one of the leaders of the pack. It's the 'difference that makes a difference' and you can see it in their body language, tone and presence. To be able to process this type of information the observer must be able to carry out an empathetic but objective assessment of the player in different scenarios and relationships. You could say that skilled assessors are able to pull the 'rabbit' out of the situation.

Developing subtler skills

Separately, the fox and the rabbit provide detailed information but together they provide more understanding of the situation at hand. Football has always relied on data but as time has gone by, the data has been targeted, specific, and more 'fox' dominant. As Mark Anderson says, 'Data was scribbling notes on the back of cigarette paper and analytics were the eyes and ears of the scout.' The scouts would record the physical outcomes and absorb the emotional analytics. They would assess the player's verbal and non-verbal communication, mood, attitude and influence within different scenarios, 'rabbit information', if you like. Money in football is increasing and scouting networks are expanding but it's important that clubs still have staff who can see and manage the 'rabbit information'.

I don't watch as many games now, as more games are being observed via video analysts. When I am at a game I look for that wow factor. I watch players who can pass, pass, pass but I look for someone who can do something different and make me say 'wow'. It's difficult to feel something that makes you say wow when watching the game on a screen. The wow factor is what it takes to play for England; elite players do elite things.

—Bob Langford
Identification Reporter for England U18 and U21

There is no specific way to develop empathic understanding and sensory acuity (sharp observation skills). However, personal development encourages you to look inwards and that is the right path. Developing who you are as a person changes how you view other people. As you change, so do the filters you use to see, hear and feel. This is something that not only scouts can utilise, but also coaches and managers in different ways. Top managers use sharp observation skills to assess how to approach each player and get the best out of them. Sir Alex Ferguson is known for this and he mentions some of his strategies in his book *Leadership*.

I was the type of player that if I wasn't performing well you'd be playing with ten men and if I was performing well, I'd win you the game. I played behind the strikers as a number ten with a mission to create opportunities. My name's Stephen Cooke, I started my professional football career at the age of nine for Walsall FC. By the age of 14 I was called up to play for England Under-15s in 1997.

Back then, if you played for England you had to attend the FA National School of Excellence in Lilleshall. So, I packed my bags to start my new life in Lilleshall alongside my international teammates that included Jermaine Defoe (Charlton Athletic FC), Leon Britton (Arsenal FC) and Leon Knight (Chelsea FC). We left our personal lives behind to increase our commitment to the game and develop our football education. During this time, I was told by a few people within the England set up that if I was going to be playing for England schoolboys, Walsall's academy was not the kind of club I should be at. There was a pressure to leave. Another player who played for Bristol City was told the same thing, but he signed a contract extension at Bristol City, his situation was slightly different to mine as Bristol City were a bigger club than Walsall. The England staff would tell me that there were a lot clubs that wanted to sign me and that I didn't need to sign there for long, just sign for two years until my 16th birthday and that I wouldn't be at the club I signed for during those two years anyway as I would remain at Lilleshall with the England team (only training at the club during school holidays).

It was a big thing for me to sign for a club that was not near home in the Midlands but because I was going to live at Lilleshall regardless of the club I was signed to, I decided to sign for Manchester United purely because they were the club I supported. Man United had been watching me from the age of 11 and I signed for them at 14. The transition from Walsall to Man United was smooth as I knew a few of the lads from the England team. I got the biggest eye-opener when I trained at Man United during the school holidays because everything was done to the highest standard. The way the staff treated you, how the club was run, the type of training we did and the standard of players I was playing with were out of this world. The difference in how I experienced football and life in general was huge.

After two years, our time in Lilleshall came to an end. My England teammates were talking about whether they would go back to their original clubs or sign for a different one. Everyone knew Defoe was leaving Charlton to go to West Ham, Britton was flirting with Aston Villa, Chelsea and West Ham. And me? Well, I wasn't sure. My contract at Manchester United was ending and they wanted me to extend but, as much as I enjoyed being at Man United, I felt overwhelmed when I was there; I felt the club was too big for me. At the time the midfield in the first team was David Beckham, Paul Scholes, Roy Keane and Ryan Giggs. I wanted to play in the first team as soon as I could and the task to dislodge one of those players seemed too big which was one of the reasons I turned down the five-year contract that was on offer. On the surface it sounds great, but during this time I found my life very stressful because I kept having to go to meetings with Sir Alex Ferguson and other members from the club who were trying to convince me to stay. They were asking why I didn't want to sign an extension and what did I want them to do so that I would sign. Although I felt the club was too big for me, my biggest problem was something they couldn't do anything about: the location. I was just a 16-year-old boy that wanted to go home. I'm from Walsall so it's not as if Sir Alex Ferguson could just relocate the club.

For this reason, I signed for the biggest club near my home at the time: Aston Villa. I made my debut in the first team when I was 17 years old at Villa Park against Celta Vigo in the UEFA Intertoto Cup, coming on as a sub to replace Julian Joachim. Unfortunately, my second appearance was delayed as Man United were demanding a fee for me and the two clubs couldn't come to an agreement on how much I was worth. This delayed subsequent appearances in the first team too, because if I played, my value would increase with every appearance. Eventually, the two clubs agreed on just over £1 million, which was a lot for a teenager back then. It was hardly spoken about at the time as my friend Jermaine Pennant had just moved from Notts County to Arsenal for £2 million, so his transfer overshadowed mine.

I was still playing for England with the likes of Michael Chopra (Newcastle United FC), Jermaine Jenas (Nottingham Forest FC) and Lionel Morgan (Wimbledon FC). After my debut in the Intertoto Cup, I had to wait two years to make my Premier League debut at 19 years old. I played a few games, signed a new three-year contract, then after I signed it I got injured during pre-season. Once I regained fitness I became captain of the reserves and went out on loan to lower league teams Bournemouth and Wycombe Wanderers.

I found playing in the lower leagues of English football different from what I was used to, it was about life and death to them while I was going there to learn. Coming through the ranks of a Premier League club had taught me to play football in a style that involves passing throughout the team, to be composed and that it was OK to receive the ball under pressure. I then went on loan to clubs that choose to do the opposite. Nothing against those clubs, but in terms of my development it didn't make sense to me. I became disillusioned, began to question myself, started wondering what this was all about. This game that I had dedicated my life to wasn't what I thought it would be. I started doing things on the pitch that didn't fit in with who I was as a player, I remember saying to myself, 'Jesus! I'm not that sort of player, this is not who I am.' I had moved away from home at 14 to commit to my dream and this was not how I imagined it. Although I didn't enjoy my time at Bournemouth I did well there. They wanted me to sign for them permanently and their reports back to Villa said that I had done exceptionally well and that I should be playing in Villa's first team.

I was 23 years old when my time at Villa came to an end. I was injured for the last 17 months of my contract. David O'Leary, the manager at the time, had never seen me play and I think he wanted me off the wage bill so he didn't offer me a new contract. I had an opportunity to sign for Walsall but this time I wanted to get away and start afresh so I took up my only other option. I went back to Bournemouth, but this time I signed on a permanent basis. My knees could only take 60 to 70 minutes of football and that was after having injections before the match and after the matches on Saturday. After the games on Saturday I couldn't walk till Monday.

I was never the same player after my injuries at Villa; the pain became unbearable and I knew that my career was going to end soon. I wasn't doing myself justice when I played at Bournemouth because my body was no longer able to handle the demands of professional football. It frustrated me because I didn't want people to remember me as a poor player or someone that just got the ball and passed it to another midfield player; I wanted to be there to create. I understand that some players do play the simple game and there's nothing wrong with that as diverse styles are needed, but I had no interest in becoming that kind of player. I wouldn't pay money to watch a player do that; I would pay money to see them do something a bit different. If I couldn't be the difference, then I didn't see the point in being there, so I retired at 26 once my Bournemouth contract expired. I wanted people to remember me as the player they saw when I was at my best, my legacy was more important than the money.

Looking back at my career I had great times: making my debut for Villa at a young age, representing my country, playing with my favourite player at youth level, Joe Cole, for England, my best player at senior level, Paul Merson, for Villa, and against my best player, Paul Scholes, who was at Manchester United. The lows included feeling pressured to sign a five-year contract at Manchester United, injury, being on loan and, ironically, not signing for Manchester United. If I had signed at Man United, the worst-case scenario would have been getting released. Getting released from Man United opens up the door to more clubs than getting released from Aston Villa. It's easily the biggest regret of my life.

—**Stephen Cooke**
former Aston Villa midfielder and
England youth international

Footballers make decisions that change their lives and their families' lives forever, from commuting to training grounds multiple times per week and moving countries to kids having to move schools or players having to leave family behind. As time goes on and scouting networks expand, more young players than ever are having to make life-changing decisions while still in school, decisions that shape their careers and their lives as a whole, decisions made without much depth to their reasoning. Cooke's example is one of many. He signed for Man United without considering what his preference would be in two years' time, what risks would come should the move not work out, and which subsequent club would offer him the best opportunities should he have to leave Man United. Being young he needed guidance on how to think effectively, but he couldn't get that guidance from any clubs because they would just tell him their club was the best option. This is where the agent comes in. Some say young kids shouldn't have an agent, but who else are they going to get advice from? The relationships within football can be smooth as a baby's bottom or as rough as a hedgehog's back. Everybody means well, but the emotional furnace of football can lead to people acting out of character.

Conflicts of interest

Club staff look out for players and try to support them as much as possible but there will always be a limit to the amount of support they can provide because sometimes the support needed is to the detriment of the club or would involve challenging a colleague, thus putting their job under threat. In Stephen Cooke's case, a Man United representative might have thought it would be in Cooke's best interests to sign for Villa, but he was employed by Man United so he was going to act in their favour. Club staff are employed by the club and so the moment they have the player's best interests at heart there is a conflict of interest. This is not a criticism of the clubs or their staff, but there needs to be clarity in this situation to prevent the continuous heartbreak and mental health problems that result from this blind relationship.

On a counselling professional development day, I began talking to a fellow counsellor about Soccology and she then shared that her son was at a professional academy. I asked her if I could relate her story and she agreed on the understanding that she, her son and the club remain anonymous.

My son was scouted at the age of nine while playing football locally. I was a little concerned about how such a young child would cope with the academy system but understandably he was delighted, and I was reassured that his welfare would be very much at the forefront, that the academy approach was well thought through and was different from club football. In some ways this was true, for example, parents were not supposed to shout from the sides unless the comments were positive. This was never fully adhered to, however, and it was, in my view, quite a demanding, aggressive and macho environment.

The commitment expected from families was huge and involved ferrying children to training twice a week, plus matches at weekends sometimes over long distances. Often parents would need to finish work early, grandparents were recruited and younger siblings had to be brought along as well which meant eating on the run, dashing through rush hour traffic and so on. This hadn't been explained in any detail when we signed and it often felt stressful. We received very little feedback despite trying to meet all these demands.

My observation was that coaches were overly focused on the physical, shouting orders at kids and sometimes were quite undermining and judgemental, considering the ages of the boys involved. I remember feeling very torn trying to balance his need to be creative and use his imagination with the demands of this very narrow physical skills training. I know many boys often felt overly anxious about getting things wrong which I now see as counter-productive in terms of them becoming confident, creative people and players. Overall, some good intentions were seriously undermined by the coaches and administrators' inadequate training in child development across the board. Despite all this my son enjoyed being part of the team and was completely committed to his football. He looked up to the coaches, but I saw first-hand how emotions had to be suppressed rather than expressed in this environment.

One of my earlier observations was that he showed flair as a footballer at a young age because he had an imaginative mind. I am very sad to say that this was squashed and narrowed by the system. Unfortunately, the coaching was very controlling and created an element of fear and anxiety making it very unlikely that these boys could think creatively. I still see the after effects over a decade later where a sensitive child was made to feel inadequate and had to hide their true personality in order to fit in. Surely with all the recent talk of diversity in football there could also be an argument for diversity of personality!

The real eye-opener came when, after a number of years, he was released. This badly-managed exit process caused the most distress. All the assurances we had been given related to emotional wellbeing were brushed aside and it was done in the most callous, unprofessional way. We received a last-minute phone call which resulted in me having to break the news to him after school, and before a training session, otherwise he would have turned up with everybody knowing except him. We had not even been invited in to meet staff or clarify things. He was distraught and in shock because a temporary manager had made the decision based on seeing him play once. This individual was unable to explain his rationale other than, 'I just don't think he's got it.'

The fact that this person had such power was unbelievable and very hard to understand. He did not seem accountable although he did leave the club shortly after and has, unsurprisingly, not progressed further. Being left with feelings of disappointment and frustration was bad enough, but what was really difficult was the sense of injustice over how everything had been communicated. The feeling that we had been unable to protect him from this one man's whim was also very hard to deal with and left a somewhat bitter taste after years of commitment and sacrifice. There seemed to be no thought for the psychological impact on the child and how they might be helped through their grief and sense of loss having tried so hard and bonded with this group of friends over a number of years.

My initial reaction was to write to people at the top, but for my son's sake I had to rein myself in and not spoil his chances of trying to play elsewhere. In fairness to other clubs he did continue to play, and the release process was handled in a more constructive way, although again suppressing emotion and 'manning up' was the norm.

Disappointments are a part of life, but it was the ignorant disregard for such a young boy's emotional development that really hurt and the academy system did not at that time seem to have any understanding of it.

I feel that a close look at the training and quality of coaches is required and I very much hope that things are beginning to change. I note that there have recently been some newspaper articles addressing the psychological impact of the academy treadmill. This debate finally seems to be moving in the right direction but many, many children have been emotionally scarred and shabbily treated by those with too much power and not enough scrutiny.

Tips to change the experience

- Structure: Have a structure in place to deal with how and when players are told difficult news.
- Group discussion: Parent and club staff should have group discussions to raise concerns, or a feedback box so clubs can find out concerns. Like players, parents can feel intimidated by club staff or scared of potentially ruining their child's chances of earning a contract. Having the option to voice their concerns anonymously or within a group (so as not to feel isolated) will help the club provide better support.

- One-to-one meetings: During player reviews (football parents' evening) the coach will tell some players they are doing well or have to improve one thing and then they are released, which leaves the players and their families wondering why. It's worth clubs doing a survey to assess the impact of their words. Afterwards staff can reflect on:
- Should we delve into more specifics about the player's game?
- Should we be brutally honest if we feel the player doesn't have a chance?
- What is it that prevents us from being honest? Worrying about hurting the player's feelings? Wanting to hang on to him to make up the numbers for the players we do want to keep?
- What is the impact of our current behaviour?
- Are we being ethical?
- How would our change in behaviour change the outcome?

Agents

An agent works solely for the player, wanting the best for them in terms of wages and career success. How do players know which agent to pick? Players often gravitate towards agents who have big-name players on their books, but this may not be the best idea. Agencies with big-name clients often don't focus as much on those of lower status or fight as much on their behalf. This is because they bring in less money or because the agent may not want to damage the relationship with their bigger client's club. (I use the term 'big-name players' to describe the popular players across first team football and youth football.)

My biggest mistake in football was turning down Northampton Town. Stuart Gray was in charge and he knew me from his time as assistant manager at Aston Villa. Gray asked me to sign for Northampton when I left QPR but instead I opted for Walsall because I wanted to be back home in Birmingham and Walsall were flying at the time. That was my biggest regret because I should have gone with the guy I knew and who knew me; he would have helped me.

I signed for Walsall, scored on my debut away to Luton after about five minutes, played about three or four games, injured my calf and once I returned to full fitness I didn't really play again and wasn't offered a new contract. It was pre-season, I was 26 years old without a club and my agent at the time told me it would be OK, not to rush and sign for anyone and to wait for the right offer. He wasn't really a football man, but great at doing deals and a really nice guy. I think because he was so wealthy he was very laid back in these intense situations, too laid back. That was another mistake I made. I think I needed an agent that knew about football, so they could dig me out when I wasn't performing. Some players don't like that, but I think it's needed.

—Stefan Moore
former Aston Villa and England international

On the flip side, an agent with big-name clients will have connections with the bigger clubs and use them effectively to manoeuvre their player a transfer. The truth is, it's difficult to analyse who will do the right thing. There is no official way to decide whether an agent is good or bad, the conclusion is subjective. My tip is to see how an agent manages their 'worst player', by that I mean the one in the worst situation, released by his club and who needs someone to ring around for him, get trials and provide emotional support. That's when a player needs an agent most. If they put the work in for their worst player, then there's a good chance the agent will be there for you too should you fall on bad times. Big-name players aren't as difficult to find work for, but they may be high maintenance, which means that the agent will have to provide emotional support when they feel hurt after being dropped, bypassed for a promotion into the team or played out of position.

There are agents who sign players and then simply wait for payday to arrive. When players notice how attentive their teammates' agents are and compare it with how they are being treated, they often decide to leave their agent and I don't blame them. But there are also agents who are treated very badly by players. There are countless stories of agents who put the work in, call around and keep trying to sell the player into a club despite continuous knock backs, until finally a club agrees to take him. The player signs for the club only to get a different agent to sign off on the deal, who is then paid for the work. (This is because an agent is not paid until they have negotiated a transfer or new contract for the player, with some taking a small percentage of the player's salary monthly.) The player stops answering the phone to his former agent and so the person that arranged the new team, was available on the other end of the phone when needed and travelled around the world to watch their games ends up getting nothing. Players will leave agents even if they have a signed agreement and only a handful of agents ever take players to court. As you might imagine, this can have a devastating effect on agents and can affect their behaviour moving forward. I have known agents that have walked away from football after having a breakdown, others have been forced to quit because the opportunity to feed their family was taken away from them and they had to find a job with a guaranteed wage at the end of the month. Others have cynically changed their approach, giving advice or negotiating player contracts in their own favour and not the player's.

An agent can become so insecure that they start following their player everywhere, afraid that another agent will try to 'steal' their player from them. The connection between agent and player is a relationship. If a player respects, commits and opens up to their agent, it will build a deeper level of connection and trust. They will be able to speak on their behalf with greater understanding and be more inclined to put in a double shift if needed. If the agent trusts the player and feels reassured they are not about to be dumped, then they will invest in the player's long-term future because their own future is linked to it. Reassuring your agent can change your career. Agents sometimes don't give everything, not because they can't be bothered or are money grabbers, but because football is a small world and they hear rumours of meetings their player has had with other agents or they pick up 'that feeling' from a change in the player's behaviour. If the agent doesn't trust the player, they will only invest in them for the short term.

Unfortunately, there is no voice for the agents. We do a lot of work for players and families, yet are still seen as villains.

—**Paolo Vernazza**
former Arsenal and England international

The role of family

Like agents and club staff, parents usually have their child's interest at heart, but some are blinded by the money-making potential involved. This affects how they help their child make decisions and the advice they may give about their future career. This is especially true if the family is struggling financially, in fact some parents are quite open about seeing their child as a pension. When they realise that their parents are seeing them as a source of money or as a player and no longer their child, it can result in the person arguing with their family or distancing themselves.

It's difficult for players because from a young age they can earn more in one week than their family does in one year and some players end up being used by their family. Football can improve this by educating players in how to manage these situations, not to tell them how to live life but how to make better life choices.

—**Gael Clichy**
former Arsenal and France international

Aside from the bigger issues like decision-making about career paths, young players need day-to-day support. This can be difficult for conscientious parents of elite children. Some worry that they are not doing enough and some that they are doing too much.

How parents can help

Ask your child how they would like to be supported.

Ask your child if they want to talk about their performance. (They may want to leave 'football' conversations at work or they may want to talk about work without being judged. This means the parent is there to listen and be the sounding board only, not to give feedback.)

Have discussions about their career while they are doing something else mentally absorbing, for example playing a computer game, cooking or fishing. The activity takes the intensity out of the situation. Some children struggle to have intense conversations because they're not used to them. They will probably never have had a parent discussing exam results, going through the answers in the car on the way home from school and analysing their exam performance.

Regularly checking in on how your child is feeling provides great comfort. Having people around that don't focus on money or performance or career allows the young player to be themselves. Players have a lot of expectations placed on them and everything revolves around what can be extracted from them. Apparently harmless questions such as, 'Are you still injured?' may have already been asked over and over by the manager and fans, they don't want to hear it at home, especially as injuries cause of a lot of stress.

Introducing someone as a player to others, for example, 'This is Emma's son, he used to play for Aston Villa,' is another issue that can cause problems. It's something proud relatives often do without knowing the discomfort it causes. Players often don't feel able to tell their relatives how they feel so their reaction is to withdraw from those people instead.

When speaking to families who have come to me independently for advice, or when I give classes to families on how to support their elite children, I have noticed that the great majority do not understand the system. My advice in this situation is to tune into the child's feelings. You may not know as much about the football system as coaches, but welfare is not about football. Be confident in supporting your child and make sure you communicate your concerns about specific situations so that you, and the club, can ensure the best outcome for the child.

> Clubs, agents and families may support the player emotionally but who develops their ability to think? That is the subject of the next chapter.

NINE

OFF-FIELD DECISION-MAKING

Clubs, agents and families may support the player emotionally but who develops their ability to think? Players must develop their ability to assess football from a career perspective because the degree of commitment required from youngsters in the game has increased dramatically. Youngsters have to make all kinds of decisions, some of which will have far-reaching effects well into adulthood. Should they leave their school and join the club's school? Is it the best time to swap clubs? Is this the best contract at this time? Is this person the best agent for them with their best interests at heart?

As we saw earlier, many are mentally unprepared to make these kinds of decisions and often base their choices on short-term emotions. Cooke moved to Manchester United because he supported the club, then he moved to Aston Villa to be back home. If he'd fast-forwarded into the future to assess the impact of his decision, he may have decided not to go to Man United at 14, but to sign for Villa instead, which would have resulted in a smoother transition into Villa's first team. He could have done the same once he signed with Manchester United and fast-forwarded two years to ask himself if he was willing to live in Manchester after he was 16. If the answer was no, he could then have tackled those complexities head on, asking himself questions like, 'How can I adapt?' He could have considered the opportunities that Man United would open up should he not be successful.

I use the term 'fast-forward' because it's something that

the players could do for themselves depending on their understanding of the game. But if their understanding of football isn't sufficient for them to make this kind of rigorous assessment, then it is important that the agent steps in to teach them how to do this. However, not many agents have this ability, even if they are former players. I've come across plenty over the last 20 years and only a handful are capable. A simple way to gauge whether an agent can fast-forward effectively is to discuss transfer news and ask for their opinion on potential moves from the angle of the rumoured player. Do they think the player should move or stay? Why? What impact would that decision have on their career in five years? What are similar examples? The more detail you go into, the better.

Just as players need to do extras to develop decision-making skills on the field, they need to do extras to develop decision-making skills off the field. I have used Cooke's story as an example because he was known as one of the best talents in the country. I know this first-hand from playing against him and, besides, there weren't many 16-year-olds that Sir Alex Ferguson went out of his way to sign. The sport lost an artist, the England team lost a great talent and, more importantly, Cooke lost the chance of a more fruitful career because he couldn't fast-forward with more clarity when he was younger.

Cookie was technically one of the best players I've seen growing up. What he lacked in physique he more than made up with in ability. His passing was top class, whether a through ball or the weight of pass, it was always perfect. Even though he wasn't quick, he had this great ability to beat players with ease and glide past them. Always looking like he had time on the ball, never panicking, the sign of a top player!

—**Leon Britton**
Swansea City and England international

The power of reputation

Football brings so much to society and means a lot to many different people, but to those that work in it, it's a job, and like all jobs it has good times and bad. During the bad times people can be deeply affected and become shadows of themselves. I've spoken to coaches, agents, players and parents who have had problems and while the stories are different, one theme stands out: communication issues through miscommunication or lack of communication.

The number of players that become blacklisted is a concern. They might fall out with a manager, so their agent tries to get them a new club only for the new club to turn them down after receiving a bad reference from the previous club. The disputes within the men's game are stereotypical. Men upset each other but rather than talking about their feelings, they try to get one up on the other person by reacting aggressively to intimidate or by trying to damage their rival's career. Sometimes the player has done something wrong, sometimes the manager has done something wrong, and sometimes the story about the player or manager is a rumour with no truth to it. Players tend to come off worse in disputes because a manager's reference about a player carries more weight than a player's reference about a manager when looking for, or trying to keep, a job.

When I went to QPR, I had five different managers between 2005 to 2008. Ian Holloway was the manager that signed me. At the time I was doing OK, not bad and not great, so I was in and out of the team, but Holloway was really good with how he managed me.

When Gary Waddock became manager, I was straight out of the squad. There were eight of us that weren't allowed to train with the team. Marcus Bignot, Marc Bircham, myself and others trained by ourselves for about six weeks. It was horrendous! He had his squad of players and didn't want us, so we had to go into work knowing that we were there just for the sake of it.

Waddock got sacked and John Gregory took over, a manager I knew well from our time together at Aston Villa. On his first day he pulled me into his office and said, 'I've heard that you've got a bad attitude, so I don't want you here. I'll give you a pay-off so go to Birmingham (where I'm from) and come back next week, by then we'll have sorted it out'. I had two years left on my contract. That would be hard to hear from anyone who hadn't taken the time to get to know me, but it was worse coming from a manager that knew me and knew me well. Gregory liked me during my time at Aston Villa; I know this because of how he engaged with me during those days and because he put me on the bench as a 17-year-old. So, to say he had 'heard' I had a bad attitude was difficult to take.

The following week I went back to the club and he told me that the club weren't going to offer me the type of pay-off I was looking for so 'let's see what happens'. We had a reserve game the next day; I played, scored a couple but cut my eye open and got a fractured cheekbone that needed 15 stitches. I went into training the next day and Gregory pulled me aside and said that he'd seen something in me and that he wasn't going to listen to anybody else. He told the fitness coach that he had three weeks to get me fit, as I couldn't train because of my facial injuries. I had to work with the fitness coach from 9:00 am to 5:00 pm every day. I got fit and worked my way back into the team again.

—**Stefan Moore**
former Ashton Villa and England international

It's important for players to be aware of stories like Stefan's because, regardless of whether the rumour is true or not, they must always be prepared to deal with the consequences. Reputations spread through the game like wildfire, killing careers.

Money problems

Football is slowly providing financial literacy training and other types of financial support, with the goal of improving the relationship footballers have with money. This is to be commended; the more support players have the better. However, poor financial management isn't generally a result of someone not knowing how to save or being unaware of the risks of excessive spending, although that may be true for some. From my experience, a player's spending issues are often emotional. Here are some of ways this can manifest:

- Keeping up with the Jones
  Trying to emulate others or not wanting to be outdone by their teammates or players from other clubs means often players stretch themselves past their contractual means. Some live in immediate debt and others take on commitments that bring future debt when they aren't offered a new contract or the new contract offer is for less than expected.
- Mama I made it syndrome
  This is the pressure of having to live up to a lifestyle that says, 'Look mama, I made it!' Whether its clothes, cars, or splurging on others, the player knows they shouldn't spend so much but the pressure to meet expectations is easier than challenging them.

  While the average 18-year-old is at college with a part-time job earning £100 or £200 pounds a week and has to decide whether or not they can afford to go to a social event, 18-year-olds at Premier League clubs earn £500 per week on average. They get into nightclubs free, are given clothes for free and get free food and drinks too in a few places (most notably at work). Attending a social event won't affect their financial state but might have more of an impact on their physical fitness and performance.

- Easy come, easy go
  Players work extremely hard physically and emotionally, the labour is intense from a young age. Yet despite the hard work and the negatives, football is a dream job; to be paid for something that you would do for free leads to players not placing the same value on money as someone who works in a job they do not enjoy. The money comes easily not because players don't work hard, but because they love what they do. Many feel rich before they are even in the position of being paid. Because the money is a bonus, they are less rigorous about how they spend it.
- Gambling
  The dad of basketball legend Michael Jordan once said that his son didn't have a gambling problem; he had a competitive problem. The intensity of an athlete's working environment is great for sport but the impact it has outside of sport is challenging for some. Being competitive is no longer a persona they adopt at work; it's who they become. Squad numbers on their kit, boots, email addresses, passwords, social media accounts and company names all contribute towards the identities of player and person merging into one. The behaviour spills over into their personal lives; they use their money and free time in the real world and the digital one to get their competitive fix – junkies hooked on the natural high of competition. Players use gambling as a way of passing time while travelling to matches or sitting at home after a short day's work. There are a host of other things they could do, but the buzz of victory engages them and gives them the feeling they crave. Of course this is not the reason why a player gambles; each person has their own unique story.
- Debt
  This can dictate the course of a footballer's career and

affect performances on the pitch as the worry of carrying the financial burden wears the player out. Debt also plays a big role in transfers. Some players will move clubs to give their career a boost, dropping down a level in club status and wage only to bounce back up again in both. But some players can't afford to drop down a level in wages because they won't be able to maintain their lifestyle, so their career moves become money driven and not career driven. The embarrassment of being in debt in a career that is so apparently lucrative traps them in silent shame.

Yes, there are conversations taking place about finances in the world of football, however, they are taking place from a distance. Players need to be encouraged to dig into their motives – to the materialism linked to keeping up with the Jones, the guilt attached to the 'mama I made it' syndrome, the detachment of the easy come, easy go, the merging of the athlete and the person – because it brings everything close to home. And the less hypothetical and more personal something is, the greater the chance for engagement, education and transformation.

The role of player personalities

One legend attached to Michael Jordan is that on the first day of a training camp he said to his teammates that he would only pass them the ball once. If they didn't do anything with it he would not give it to them again because he could miss a shot on his own and he could misplace a pass on his own. The story was an example of how Jordan tested his teammates to see what they could do with a ball in a pressurised environment. Were they going to give it away, give it back to him in fear or were they going to make something happen? How were they going to manage?

Players are under a lot of pressure from themselves, their family, the club, the fans and the media. This affects the decisions they make on the pitch from showing for the ball to receive possession to turning down a calculated risk and taking the easier option. At times it's difficult to see how players are affected because some put on a brave face and internalise their feelings, which then damages their performances.

As I mentioned earlier, Training Ground International (TGI) is a term my friends and I coined for players who would train like Maradona during the week, only to play like Madonna on a Saturday; players who had the ability to perform but couldn't do so because of psycho-emotional stumbling blocks. Although players have different names for it (or may not even name it or notice it at all), TGI is common in football.

When I first went to Charlton as a 14-year-old, I struggled to be the best version of myself because I was looking for a transaction to support my emotional needs. I wanted to do something good and, in return, receive praise or acknowledgement to empower my performance. The praise and acknowledgement never came, but anxiety and performance insecurity did, and I became a shadow of my former self.

It is easier to be praised in training than it is in a match. In training, the coach focuses on development and problem solving and individuals get personal attention when something is flagged. Something as simple as a player in possession, turning and passing the ball across the pitch can receive great praise from a coach if that was the theme during his session. But in a match a player can perform the same action throughout the game and the coach may say nothing because he's focusing on the team as a whole unit.

Football starts in the head and finishes on the pitch, I create a fantasy in my mind then I transfer it to the pitch. Feelings are everything in football. If I have a bad feeling I cannot give 100 per cent on the pitch because it messes with my head, where football starts.

—**Filston Mawana**
Hoffenheim and Sweden international

Filston describes how his ability to create images in his mind and make decisions on the pitch can be hijacked by negative feelings, which stop him performing. Players are subjected to positive and negative feelings within the game, and how and if you process these will determine the effects they have on you. Some players have the personality to absorb the positive, see the negative for what it is and let it go. If something doesn't feed into them positively they don't absorb it. It's a powerful skill and an effective way of managing self. Their self-confidence and desire to succeed outmuscles the pressure and criticism of others.

Wayne Rooney's first Premier League goal was for Everton against Arsenal; he drew the ball out of the sky, turned around, took a couple of touches towards goal and bent the ball into the top corner. There were three key parts to that goal: first, he didn't try to head the ball; second, he turned down the opportunity to play the ball to more senior players; and third, he chose a difficult shot. The safe option would have been to strike through the ball (smash it), but he went for the more technically challenging option of curling it into the corner. Other players of Rooney's age in the same situation – playing against one of the best teams in Europe at 16 years old – might have been aware of the options and been capable of the execution, but the enormity of the situation might have resulted in them choosing the safe option.

Decision-making is one thing, the other is a high level of self-belief; a resilient self-belief which stays intact even when intensely challenged. The kind of self-belief that Andrea Pirlo needed when his teammates in the Brescia youth team refused to pass to him and their parents accused him of thinking he was Diego Maradona. A self-belief that starts with positive self-talk and develops into positive behaviour on the pitch. Players can help support their mind and their actions on the pitch by using both their internal voice (their inner coach) and their physical voice. A good tip is to behave as though you are the best and 'speak things into existence'.

Craig Bellamy was cheeky, chirpy and had an arrogance about him on the pitch that was part of his identity as a player.
—**Kevin James**
former Charlton Athletic and Nottingham Forest midfielder

'Shut up or I'll flick the ball over your head!' Jerome Thomas is having an aggressive exchange with my right back Jermaine St Luce. Moments later Jerome receives the ball 30 yards from our goal on the left wing, flicks the ball over Jermaine's head, takes a touch towards goal and from 25 yards out, BANG! The ball zooms straight into the top corner. He scores.

I played against Jerome in District Football and afterwards, when Arsenal bought him from Luton Town. As youth team players and young professionals, we faced each other a lot over the years and I got to know Jerome off the field. He projected a self-belief that was sky high, a self-belief that shaped his personality on and off the field, a self-belief that assisted his performances and led him to being seen as one of the best left-wingers in youth football. When you have talent and you tell yourself and the world that you are the best, something within you changes. Your performance improves as a result of the affirmation. When discussing this type of player Anthony Gardner uses the term 'football arrogance', a term I now use regularly as well. The word 'arrogance' is often used negatively, however, we are using this term neutrally to describe a player who has a strong belief in their own ability.

I have used Jerome as an example because he was an extroverted player who was easy to identify, but what about introverted players? Can they have football arrogance too?

In September 2016, I worked with two groups at Arsenal, the Under-16s and a mix of Under-18s and young professionals. The Under-16 group consisted of ten players; they were quiet, considerate of each other when they spoke and mindful of others in their view of the world. I was impressed by the maturity of Reiss Nelson, a player I knew of because of his performances for Arsenal and England at youth level. He was reserved, calculated and spoke when he could add something to help the conversation, or challenge it if he felt it was going in the wrong direction. The second group consisted of a mixture of 15 Under-18s and young professionals; players who were creating waves with their performances for Arsenal and England at youth level, the likes of Eddie Nketiah, Joe Willock, Josh Da Silva and Marcus McGuane. Marcus, like Reiss, was more reserved while the others were boisterous and bounced off each other.

Fast-forward to March 2016. I went to Manchester City to work with a few of their youth teams. Man City beat most teams and had the second-best youth system in the country according to coaches in the game, with Chelsea rated as the best. In the Man City Under-16 team of 2016 (there were Under-15s in the room too), more than half had been bought from other clubs. The talent in the room was unstoppable on the pitch.

Before the session started there was the usual technical drama I have at every club when I try to connect my laptop to the club's system. While the club staff were assisting me,

I made small talk with the players. I learnt that they had given a team a hiding the week before; one of them, Tyrese Campbell, son of former Arsenal and Everton striker Kevin Campbell, had scored a hat-trick. I asked him how many goals he had for the season; he told me 40. It was only March and he already had numbers on par with Lionel Messi and Cristiano Ronaldo!

Tyrese had a strong personality and could hold his own in the group, but Phil Foden and Jadon Sancho were the two most prominent personalities in the room. They were the ones considered to have the most promise and I noticed that the team felt that too demonstrated by how they behaved, particularly in response to Jadon. While Phil spoke with confidence, shrugging off fear of judgement, Jadon took it to the next level sharing his views about others even when the comments were risky. He had a strong influence over the group; when he spoke others listened intently, giggled on cue and murmured agreement when he said things they were thinking themselves but were not brave enough to say. Jadon reminds me of Jerome Thomas in both skills and attitude.

You need that intense confidence. When I play I have that; you need it. I tell players during a game, 'You ain't doing nothing against me today, you ain't telling me nothing, you ain't going past me. Nothing. I'm tha man!'

I tell people all the time, 'Football is a collective sport. If you don't win your individual battles you will get run over and then it becomes a collective problem'. For example, if you're playing left back and the right winger you're up against goes past you like you're not even there, your team will be under pressure. Jordan Rhodes was one of the least technical players I've played with, but he would always score goals because he had great confidence and belief in himself.

There are people that are 'ballers' and there are people that are 'footballers'. 'Ballers' are players that play in a skilful or technical way;

'footballers' are functional, they get the job done. Jordan is a footballer and on the flip side, there's Juan Pablo Pino, he's a baller. I played with Juan Pablo Pino at Galatasaray. He could easily have been one of the top ten players in the world, but he just didn't care. He could use both feet, scoring with either from 30 yards out into the top corner and going past players like they weren't there. I wouldn't say that he didn't have confidence, but he didn't have that grit, that need to win regardless, because he was getting paid anyway. He had come from nothing, from living in a favela in Columbia, so in his eyes he'd already made it, he wasn't thinking about being the best player. If he had that confidence, that arrogance, that Cristiano Ronaldo mentality, he would be a problem for oppositions everywhere.

Players don't need to have super confidence to make it, or even be successful, as hundreds of players have shown. But super confidence is what makes the difference between those just having a good career and those that reach the top.

—**Colin Kazim-Richards**
Corinthians and Turkey international

I've seen the players from both groups play and have worked with them in a classroom setting. I would class Tyrese Campbell, Phil Foden, Reiss Nelson and Marcus McGuane as reserved and Eddie Nketiah, Joe Willock, Josh Da Silva and Jadon Sancho as having football arrogance. They are all at different levels within those categories but all successful in their careers so far. They all made their first team debuts in professional football before the age of 19 for Europe's finest clubs. Campbell moved to Stoke City, McGuane to Barcelona and Sancho to Dortmund.

Using this group of players as a case study shows that there is no set formula, no set character trait that is needed to make it to the top. Commercially, the more reserved approach of Campbell, Foden, Nelson and McGuane is preferred and better received, but if you took away the boisterous side of

Nketiah, Willock, Da Silva and Sancho, you wouldn't have players performing to the same high standard.

Player personality is not just about performance, it's about managing your career as a whole. There are many different types of successful player and many things to take into consideration. Although there's an expectation that players should be humble, it doesn't work for everyone; having a low estimation of their own importance doesn't support the 'football character' of some players.

One day, someone said to me, 'You're a very good player, the problem is you're a Jack of all trades but master of none.' That hurt me. The thing is if you're capable of playing in other positions, you're in a lose-lose situation and you won't progress as much as you should do playing in multiple positions. But if you say to the manager that you don't want to play in other positions, your attitude gets questioned, which is a shame because I should be able to decide against playing out of position without judgement. If I play, I'll be judged by my manager and everybody else when I'm playing in a position which is not my strongest.

I do think the game has changed slightly. Teams now have a body of players that multitask, but it's the specialists that dominate the key positions.

—**Colin Kazim-Richards**
Corinthians and Turkey international

Balance is vital for success. Colin's dilemma over taking one for the team is shared by thousands of players. They want to help the team but not to the detriment of their career or development. In this case, I tell them to ask themselves, 'How can I get my point across without offending the other person and compromising myself further than I am willing to go?' Every situation is unique and so is the response. Asking yourself that question will highly reduce the chance of conflict.

Neuro-Logical Levels

The terms 'world class' and 'flop' are frequently bandied about. I've always wondered how the conclusion of 'flop' is reached so easily. I see great players transfer from one team to the next; no longer hitting the heady heights they once did, losing form which never returns. Form is affected by a host of things including confidence, anxiety, limiting beliefs and environment. Some players will have a temporary dip or improvement in one or more of these elements while others have long-term twists in their career tale. I am always curious how and why form changes. Is there a relationship between elements of form? And if a relationship can be found then how can it be used to predict outcomes, for example whether a new signing will become a success? At times I get the full story, which helps me to join the dots. At other times, when I can't get the inside track, rather than just wondering, I put the limited information I have through an alignment model called Neuro-Logical Levels.

Neuro-Logical Levels (of change) is a model influenced by anthropologist Gregory Bateson, who fused the study of cybernetics and human relationships to gain a greater understanding of the psychology of individuals and groups and their functional and dysfunctional systems. In terms of football, Bateson's approach could be used to identify the elements behind a player's – or team's – form, whether good or bad and provide necessary solutions. Neuro-Linguistic Programming contributor Robert Dilts further developed Bateson's work which led to the creation of Neuro-Logical Levels (NLL). NLL refers to the process of alignment between different aspects within a system. Whether you are talking about an individual or a group, each 'system' consists of a set of processes, including values, thoughts and behaviours. These processes or elements can be used to identify a problem and/or a solution. Tweaking the model slightly, I use NLL to identify if a player or team will be 'top potential', 'flop' or 'world class'.

NLL has the potential to solve many of football's big problems by assessing whether a potential signing will be a success or not and identifying the changes needed to ensure success. Looking at both internal and external factors, the model holds the person central to the outcome. There isn't a 'one hit wonder' or magic pill to success, there are many factors on many levels. To the untrained eye, a player 'flops' when they do not perform to a set of expectations. On a deeper level the problem is more complex.

NLL is an effective model when deciding who to sign, or to identify a problem and provide a solution. For a system to be successful, all the working parts need to be in alignment; the beauty of this model is its ability to highlight and/or predict when a player or team is performing well or not based on their alignment. Alignment predicates/indicates that they are performing well and misalignment that they are not.

The NLL model is made up of the following levels:

- **Purpose** – The bigger system, family, community and spirituality. Mission in life.
- **Identity** – Self-actualisation. Who am I?
- **Beliefs & Values** – Reasons behind the behaviour. Why you do what you do.
- **Skills** – Skills drive behaviour through personalised strategies. How you do things.
- **Behaviours** – Actions and reactions. What happened?
- **Environment** – External conditions. Where and who with?

Imagine every level as a brick, one stacked on top of the other, with **Environment** at the bottom and **Purpose** at the top. Each brick needs to be in alignment to stop the whole lot tumbling down.

One way to use this model is to identify weaknesses. Let's say a striker's conversion rate on their weaker foot from within the 18-yard box is 15 per cent compared with 80 per cent when using their stronger foot. This is a problem with skills in our model. As the **Skills** brick isn't fully balanced, it sticks out slightly, making it easy to spot and also makes the whole tower of bricks unstable.

This brings us to another way to use the model: you can proactively align the levels through development to ensure maximum performance potential. Continuing with the brick analogy, in order to ensure a strong tower that can weather the storms (i.e. internal and external pressures) you need to make sure you have a strong base.

- Starting from the bottom and working up, look at the striker's **Environment**, for example: Where is he training? How often? Who is there to coach/help/support him?
- Going up a level to **Behaviours**: How is he training? What is he actually doing? What could he do differently?
- Keep moving up. What **Skills** does he already have? What is he lacking that would benefit him?

These are all transactional levels. As we move up, we enter the magical place of transformation.

- Look at **Beliefs and Values**. Why is he playing the game? What's important to him? Does he even believe he can do it?
- Regarding his **Identity**, does he see himself as a successful player or in a successful team?
- And ultimately what's the bigger pay-off? What is the **Purpose**?

Any shifts made at these transformational levels allow you to go back down and reassess the where, what and how, to make the most impactful changes.

Religious war

The marriage between Dennis Bergkamp and Inter Milan was not as fruitful as it could have been. So, what was behind him not being able to reach his potential at Inter? Bergkamp mentions in his book *Stillness and Speed* that the problem was a difference in how he and the club thought football should be played.

Inter Milan's local rivals, AC Milan, were producing wonders across Europe at the time with Arrigo Sacchi at the helm. The team was led by Dutch legends Marco Van Basten, Ruud Gullit and Frank Rijkaard. Using attack as a way to defend, AC Milan began to change how people saw football in Italy, including their local rivals Inter. Wishing to replicate the AC Milan way, Inter acquired similar ingredients in the form of Dutch players Dennis Bergkamp and Wim Jonk. The cultural shift was a big deal for a club like Inter who have a strong history of the *Cantenaccio* ('the door bolt'), a defensive style that brought success under Helenio Herrara; this success led to his Inter being referred to as *Grande Inter*. Inter's new approach was the reverse of that tradition, a change that caused upset. Bergkamp and Jonk had no idea that they were walking into a war between Inter's past and its potential future. It was a conflict that ran so deep it was referred to as the Religious War.

Bergkamp was told by Inter Milan that they were going to change their approach from a defensive style to an attacking one. The problem was that Bergkamp was born and bred in Holland, within the Ajax system, a club famed for their fluid attack. Inter Milan managers Osvaldo Bagnoli and

Giampiero Marini, on the other hand, were from Italy, a country famed for its watertight defending. You couldn't get a starker contrast between the two nations. Bergkamp and the two Inter managers had a different interpretation of attack that was linked to the culture they grew up in, and they had strong beliefs and values about different things. It would be too simple to label Bergkamp a 'flop' at Inter Milan; he was a top prospect coming out of the Ajax system, performed well in the first team, went to Inter Milan and 'flopped', then went to Arsenal going on to be, arguably, one of their best transfers ever.

Let's use NLL to explain why Bergkamp didn't reach his full potential in the black and blue of Inter Milan. Our beliefs and values underpin why we do what we do and how we think things should be done; they are our personal motivation and source of direction. This is where Bergkamp's misalignment was; a clash with his beliefs and values, represented in the style of play, meant that Bergkamp had to change how he did things and how he thought, which affected how he played. Using more energy to defend, covering more distance and having less possession took away from his role as an attacker, so he attacked less, shot less and scored less. This in turn affected his state, decisions and, ultimately, his outcome.

Moving to England and playing for Arsenal alone didn't solve Berkamp's problem. In fact, it may have brought a different problem as the game was fast-paced, less about possession and more direct than it would have been in Holland. Although he had a brief spell under Arsenal manager Bruce Rioch, his ten years of success are linked to the correlation of beliefs and values that he and Arsene Wenger both shared. Attacking, flowing football allowed Bergkamp and his teammates to roam free.

Attacking football is subjective, however, an in-depth conversation can help ensure everyone is on the same page.

If Inter or Berkgamp had used NLL, there would have been clarity before the transfer. Club and player would have seen that the move was not going to be beneficial to either party. This may have led Bergkamp to transfer to Real Madrid instead; they were also interested in the Dutchman's services during his time at Ajax.

'Flops' fall victim to misalignment and the same rule applies to teams. I have used the Neuro-Logical Level model to explain the reason behind Bergkamp's unsuccessful stint at Inter, which he supports in his book. I am aware that when I come to conclusions without working directly with the team or player, no matter how much information I have, I do not know the full story. However, like data, NLL has its place. Filtering information through Neuro-Logical Levels enables staff to assess the individual or team, identifying strengths and weaknesses, and where, when and how to apply an intervention. Neuro-Logical Level not only saves time, money and stress, it brings understanding, knowledge and success for personal and professional performance.

> As we have seen, nothing can be examined in isolation; the places and people we are exposed to play a huge role in shaping outcomes. Motivational speaker Jim Rohn famously said that we are the average of the five people we spend the most time with. In the final chapter we are going to consider the importance of the environment, and how to positively effect change.

TEN

POWER OF THE ENVIRONMENT

Christian Vieri, Alvaro Recoba and Ronaldo were at Inter during my time there. It's not like England, before training we would be told not to tackle them and not to touch them. What I loved in England is that you are close to the first team, you can talk with the first team players and that feeling was very nice for the younger players like myself back then. In Italy this doesn't happen; the first team is God, you cannot talk to them, you cannot touch them. I loved the English way, one family.
—**Raffaele Buondonno**
former Inter Milan striker and Charlton Athletic loanee

The football environment is made up of facilities and people; take the people away and all you are left with are buildings and football pitches. Facilities play an important role in what happens on the pitch and can help improve skills, but it's people and experiences that create transformation. Being exposed to models of excellence provides a host of benefits to young players coming through.

My first experience of full-time football was with West Ham United FC. The coaches were not sure if they were going to give me a full-time contract, so I needed to prove myself. I was desperate to make an impact every day, despite my uncertain contract situation. I was overwhelmed by a host of feelings that I still cannot identify even now.

Arriving early on my first day at the Chadwell Heath base, I didn't know what to do. Two months earlier I had been training for just a couple of hours in the evenings, now I was here for the day. I got changed and sat in the changing room and when players started to arrive, I ventured out around the building a bit more, joining the group on the indoor AstroTurf which also had some gym machines. One of the first players from the first team I saw was Ian Wright and his jaw hit the floor when he saw me. At the time he was married to my second cousin Debra Wright and didn't know that I played football. He would see me at his house or a family event on the odd occasion, but he wasn't expecting to see me at the training ground. His reaction was priceless!

Being able to talk now and again to a senior player like Ian made settling in a little easier for me, because he was someone familiar in the unknown world of full-time football. But it was the comedy show of Neil 'Razor' Ruddock and Paolo Di Canio that made a huge difference and helped distract from the pressure. They were like Laurel and Hardy, always taking the mickey out of each other and putting on a show for us youngsters and I will always appreciate them for that. Frank Lampard, on the other hand, didn't speak to us at all. He would sit at the same table or walk past you as though you weren't even there, which made me feel a little awkward.

Seeing the first team on a daily basis added an aspect of reality to the journey: I could see my target every day and copy positive behaviour. I was impressed by Rio Ferdinand's jovial behaviour inside the building – he would dance to house music and screech in excitement every time a new tune was mixed in – as well as his aggressive work ethic on the pitch. I'd never seen that before and it taught me that you could work hard and have fun.

Joe Cole could keep a tennis ball up using the back of his shoulder. He tied hoops to the top corners of the goal to practise and his accuracy was mind blowing. He taught me to set high standards for myself and to think outside the box when working.

Tony Carr, who was in charge of the youth team, told us that West Ham manager Harry Redknapp was going to walk over to watch us train and that we should think of his every glance as an opportunity. In fact, Redknapp did walk over to watch us a few times that pre-season. I thought I had put a hundred per cent into training before, but when Redknapp was there I found more energy from somewhere. Because a Premier League manager was taking the time to watch me play, I instantly placed more value on myself and felt relevant being there.

Seeing a clearer pathway towards the first team, I moved to Charlton that same pre-season. I had Clive Mendonca giving me one-to-one advice on financial literacy, Keith Jones giving me tips on how to improve my game, and the likes of Chris Powell and Eddie Youds providing unintentional mentoring. I was incredibly fortunate because Charlton were in the Premier League at the time, the best league in the world. When you're getting advice from models of excellence, it's priceless. In any area of life, business or sports, if you were to pay for the time of the top people to give you advice, it would cost thousands.

As a youngster at Manchester United we were always near the first team, whether it was on the training field or in the canteen at lunchtime, everyone knew each other at the club and it was a priority for Sir Alex to have a family environment. When the first team were training I could always see them and it made me hungry because every day I could see where I wanted to be. The perfect source of motivation.

—**Kieran Richardson**
former Manchester United and England international

Mentorship in football comes through studying the

behaviour and words of models of excellence. These models are usually at a more senior level than those they are mentoring, for example, the first team staff and players are models for the Under-23 team, the Under-23 team are models for the Under-18 team and so on. They motivate, teach, lead by example and inspire the up-and-coming generations, something that former Inter Milan striker Raffaele Buodonno enjoyed while in England during the 2000/2001 season.

In England in around 2005, an unfortunate trend began. Clubs opted to use separate training grounds for their teams; the youth to Under-23 teams trained in a different location to the first team. Cutting off access like this has resulted in the younger players losing invaluable relationships, lessons, experiences and potential careers. In the past, when the youth team trained at the same location as the first team it created accidental opportunities. Young players would be called over to train with the first team just before or during a training session to fill a gap. The first team manager would then request that the player stay with the first team and the rest is history.

Building your own environment

Before entering the professional game, I had the pleasure of having in my circle of friends: Craig Rocastle, Gavin Tomlin and Kevin James. We four boys lived less than half of a mile from each other. Kevin James had been in the professional environment before we began to meet up and train together, but the four of us really became professional footballers by conditioning ourselves using the power of the environment we created. Although former Chelsea and Celtic defender Paul Elliott CBE is Kevin James' second cousin and former Arsenal and Chelsea legend David Rocastle is Craig's first cousin,

Kevin and Craig, like Gavin and myself, were dependent on the group to make progress on their football journey. We created a successful environment by being available, training intensely, setting high standards for training, not shying away from giving or receiving constructive criticism and sharing a passion for football.

Millions want to be professional but only a small number are willing to do what it takes and more, so what was behind Kevin James joining Charlton at 15, Craig Rocastle signing for Chelsea at 21, Gavin Tomlin singing for Brentford at 22 and me signing for Charlton at 16?

Here are our individual accounts of the past:

How did we know what to do?
'Football was one component of us hanging together but not the only component. Kevin George and I went to primary school together before we played for a team. We went to different secondary schools – me going to Forest Hill Boys and Kevin going to Sedgehill where he would eventually meet Craig Rocastle and Kevin James who were two and three years older respectively. We came from the same area – our homes were all within a half-mile radius – and had common interests. Kevin James was a key component in our group because by the time it formed he was already playing for Charlton Athletic FC, so we had access to someone who was in the professional environment. He transferred information to us unconsciously via his attitude: how he would talk to us about what was required and how he trained. We used that information and expanded on it, creating a professional environment in how we went about "everything football". We were so dedicated, which was partly down to having nothing else to distract us (not that other things were not available), we just wanted to play football.

'From the age of nine I didn't want to be anything other than a footballer. We competed against each other in everything we did, motivated by pride, ambition and wanting to avoid being the butt of the jokes. Feedback was intense and to the point. You had to have thick skin although there was not one time where my friends critiqued my performance that I didn't like. I can certainly recall others coming to join us, never to return!' – **GT**

'We all had a competitive nature. Everybody else wanted to be footballers but they weren't willing to do what it takes. We let nothing get in our way; everything we did was valid. If one of us did something that wasn't good it wouldn't go down too well which meant that I made sure everything I did was of a high standard, so I could walk away feeling that I was ready for tomorrow. The training we did kept me in tune and was how I groomed myself into what I wanted to become. We met up to play football at the drop of a hat; there was no schedule. For years we played football together throughout the week because it was our priority.' – **CR**

'It didn't matter if we were playing football on the street or playing in the adventure playground, losing was never an option. This set my attitude towards football. When I signed for Charlton, my first professional team, it was easy to transmit my professional experience to my three friends because they all had a natural desire to push boundaries, to be fitter, win and be better than the others. The sessions we did as a group were highly intensive and competitive, each of us trying to keep the ball the longest and show the others how good we were. We took it very seriously, in fact I cannot think of anything else we took more seriously. This process pushed us through boundaries for example, going from being an OK player to being a good player, from being a good player to being a really good player, never settling.

Those competitive moments were vital. We imitated our parents' traits, growing up and being in their company a lot, we saw them surviving regardless and always offering their best efforts. Seeing how all our parents hustled rubbed off on us, there's no way we could take it easy when working towards our dream job.' - **KJ**

'The expectation was high so taking it easy was never an option during any session we had with each other. We did keep ball 90 per cent of the time and those sessions were quicker than most professional teams I have played at.' - **KG**

What tips can you give players?
'I used to have notes of what I had to do before each game. For example, one of my notes was based on my targets; when I played on right wing, one of my targets was to get ten crosses into the box per half. Whether you're trying to get into the professional game or you're already in it, it's important to study the game, study yourself and see how you can alter your game to be as effective as possible. I had between eight and ten trials before I got signed. My confidence wasn't knocked because I loved playing football, whether it was professional or non-league, and that was the most important thing to me. When I was playing for non-league football, I knew that if didn't become a professional, I would be able to earn a living playing non-league football, so I was already winning. There's a difference between loving football and loving to be a professional, some people love the game regardless, they just love playing it and others love what they can get from the game. If you want to become a professional, you must love it because the game will test you at times. If you love the game, you will pull through and if you don't then you falter. I remember going to Craig's house and not understanding how to watch football, then one day shortly after turning 16

it clicked. I realised what Craig was talking about, how the player received the ball, passing safe side etc. Before I used to just watch the match as entertainment and not as a learning tool. Study football!' – **GT**

'I used to have a football journal, after every game I'd rate myself, write about my performance and reflect over a month, half a season and a season.' – **KJ**

'Be brave enough to challenge your coach; be skilled enough to challenge your coach in the right way. If you feel that you are being mistreated, don't accuse the coach of anything, give them the responsibility by asking them questions to justify their behaviour. I would say work as hard as you can; if you are not knackered during and after training you haven't worked hard enough. This will mean taking five seconds during a training session to get your breath back as you slowly build your fitness up. During a game you will have to be more tactical with your energy levels but after a while you'll be able to repeatedly burst throughout games. When I reached 19 my recovery was instant after a sprint, I didn't feel tired. The perfect example of this is Ashley Cole; he was non-stop. Once your fitness is on point, your senses sharpen, and your technique is more precise as you are more alert.

'For those who want to get into football I say do whatever it takes. I researched where Charlton trained, what day and time my age group trained and lied to get a trial. I begged my brother to speak to the father of his girlfriend (who was a coach at Millwall) to get me a trial at Millwall. Then I was scouted by West Ham scout Dave Goodwin, the scout that had taken Rio Ferdinand to West Ham. Dave kept saying that he was going to take me to West Ham but never did or maybe I was impatient. I researched where the training ground was, what time my age group trained, and a reference name to use once the coaches asked me who sent me in. I was not willing to wait for someone to give me an opportunity, I was looking to take one and take one I did. I signed a professional contract at 17 years old at Charlton, who rejected me at 14, when the average age to sign a professional contract is 18.' – **KG**

Did you have any surprises when you entered the professional game?

'When I entered the professional game, I had disappointments over the style of play some of my managers made us use. Before I was a pro, I thought that everyone at a professional level had a certain level of understanding the game. When I became professional and saw how some people played I couldn't understand it. How could they be pros and have the top facilities, the infrastructure – everything – yet not understand the game? This led to me, and others, not playing football the way we wanted to play the game. It was not how I envisioned it. I envisioned professional football to be composed of players wanting to, and being capable of, playing football in a composed passing style.

'During my career when I went to teams that suited my style of football, I did well. Whenever things were not working out for me it was either that I needed to work harder or I needed to leave. When I went to Dagenham and Redbridge under John Steele, it was never going to work as he likes a long direct style of play. After six months at Dagenham I went to John and told him that I liked him as a person, but I didn't think our styles matched. I went on loan to Torquay United FC. At the end of the season John and myself played cat and mouse. He said that he didn't want me to leave because if he had said that, then I would have been able to leave cheaply or on a free and he wanted the most money he could get from my transfer. And although I wanted to leave I didn't say so because the club would then have asked for a transfer fee for me. Six months later I signed for Gillingham and I did well, because the Gillingham manager allowed me to play football in my preferred style. I play my best when managers allow me to express myself.' – **GT**

'I remember becoming a professional and thinking "is this it?" I had a competitive nature and wanted to be the best that I could be, but I was playing with others that really didn't give a sh*t. This is where the love for the game kicks in. If I hadn't been in love with football I would have been one of those players who didn't give their all and end up getting released. But I couldn't do that, I loved the game too much. A lot of people get into a comfort zone of, "I'm here and I have two years, so I'll pull my finger out when I want." I was surprised at the amount of mediocre mindsets there were within the game. There were players who weren't interested in promotions or winning games, they were more interested in planning their holidays. Most players liked the status of being there rather than actually being there to do a job. It really p*ssed me off!' – **CR**

'I was surprised at the high standards I saw. I thought my competitive nature was high until when I went into Charlton and saw how Kevin Nicholls tackled, he would take people out. There would be one player that was exceptional at passing, and another who was a great dribbler. The bar was raised in different elements of the game and I needed to step up.' – **KJ**

'I was surprised at the standard of players once I entered the professional game, at both ends of the scale. Some players blew my mind with their natural talents and others had me wondering how they got there.' – **KG**

Hearts and minds

'Character, whether it is instilled by parents, friends or is self-developed, is what makes the difference, regardless of the environment you are in. When I played for Yeovil Town FC we had a group of Tottenham players that joined on loan: Jonathan Obika, Steven Caulker, Ryan Mason, Andros Townsend. I don't know if it was their coach or the culture at Tottenham, but they were teenagers with attitudes more professional than the older professionals at Yeovil. They were out before training started doing extra training and prehab, last in after training had finished doing extra training and doing an extra warm down. They didn't come to Yeovil with the attitude of thinking they were better than Yeovil, they continued to do everything thoroughly. After training they would go to sleep and do another gym session in the evening because they understood what they were there for: their development. They saw Yeovil as a platform that they were going to take advantage of in order to get to where they wanted to be. They were never planning to stay at Yeovil or play at that level, so they put the work in to give themselves the best chance possible. They had come from a Premier League team to a League One team, their mentality was that League One was not their level and they were right because all except Obika ended up playing Premier League football and for the England national team. This is no coincidence.

'When I was younger I never understood what people meant when they said football was about your heart and mentality, as far as I was concerned I could play well and that was enough. Now I understand. Players would absorb lessons better if they could be taught them rather than told them.

'I remember playing centre midfield for Crawley Town FC and having a terrible game, the fans were giving me a hammering. I set up two goals and we won. Jimmy Dack who was Crawley's Assistant Manager at the time, came over to me and said that he loved my courage because a lot of people would have crumbled in my situation and no matter how many times I lost the ball, I went and got it again. I told him that was all I knew, I didn't know how to go hiding. I loved football too much to hide in games. The grounding I got from the 'keep ball' sessions we four used to do as a group helped hone my skill at managing the ball in tight spaces, which fed my confidence to keep going regardless of what happens.' – **GT**

'Signing for Chelsea was a gift and a curse. The gift was being at a place full of talent that I could learn from, the curse was leaving. Mick McGiven at Chelsea was structured but allowed you to play. Going to Sheffield Wednesday and being told to hit the ball into the corner and run box-to-box was like a dagger in the heart. They never saw the best of me because I didn't enjoy it. I gave everything I could, but happiness would have allowed me to give more. I didn't enjoy my football until I went to Europe because in England I would be told that I had been brought in, along with one or two others, because the club wanted to play a patient passing style. After losing two or three games it was "here we go again"; the manager would ask us to kick, head and run. If you were a defender who liked to just head the ball or a striker happy to flick the ball on or run in behind, then England was a great place to play, but playing in midfield was tough. It was tough to adjust to the different style of play and tough to adjust to the lies the coaches would tell to sign you. Whether they wanted to sign me on loan or sign me permanently, coaches would say to me, "We need you to get it down and play, Rocs."

'Once I signed, I would go through games hardly touching the ball because of their instructions to the team. They knew

I wouldn't have gone with them if they had told the truth, so they lied, which didn't make sense because I became no different to what they already had. How do I know they lied? The coaches would eventually get me in the office and say, "We just don't have the players to do it." I would respond by saying, "You do have the players to do it, you just don't believe in it." When I stepped into Sheffield Wednesday it was a place for Premier League rejects: myself from Chelsea, Chris Brunt from Middlesbrough, Glen Whelan from Manchester City, Stephen Maclean from Rangers, Jon-Paul McGovern from Celtic and loads more. Everybody had been taught at decent clubs. How could the coach turn around and say he didn't have the players to do it?

'My Oldham Athletic FC manager used to talk about what type of player he was and how good he had been. I know he was a very good player because I grew up watching him. But when we lost three games, he became a "hang it" merchant (kick it up the pitch), it was quite depressing. I had to retrace my steps and ask myself what had got me here. I would literally say, "I am retracing my steps to try to get myself in the mindset of having the same eagerness before entering the game in the hope that it will get through playing the long ball game." Reprogramming my mind worked but never lasted a season. There were loads of times when I didn't do enough because I was feeling sorry for myself and carrying too many emotions about how I felt the game should be played. Going into Europe allowed me to play the game how I believed it should be played. I talk to the kids that I coach in Kansas about everything Soccology is about and how their environment is fundamental. Even though I had both parents at home supporting every decision I made, if I hadn't had Gavin Tomlin, Kevin James and Kevin George around me, I would not have blossomed. I remember the four of us sitting in my room; Kevin James and Kevin George were both signed up at professional clubs, Gavin Tomlin, who was the youngest, and myself were not. They were talking about which position I could play to give me the best opportunity of breaking into the system and giving me constructive criticism. I was very argumentative (and still am) but without the feedback from my circle telling me how it is, I wouldn't have been able to mould myself.

'The game will not be nice to you, nor will life for that matter, so you have to face your truths, both positive and negative, whether you want to or not. If you don't look in the mirror you will be held back and there won't be a successful outcome. If you do face your negative truths, then you have a chance to overcome them and be successful. Your truths play out one way or another, facing them greatly increases your ability to point your outcome in the direction you would like to go. In my circle of friends there were a lot of home truths at any given moment, whereas other players we knew had plenty of people around them praising them for being talented and in a professional team, but they had no one giving constructive criticism. The player was in a bubble, thinking they could do no wrong and living out a lie. This couldn't happen in our circle, we would tell each other: "You could have done better," or, "Get your head out of your arse". Whatever needed to be said was said, it was from a good place and we moved on. Without being surrounded by my friends, my career would not have happened.' – **CR**

'I was fortunate to have Terry Westley as a coach in the youth team, he coached us in a way that was structured but we were allowed to express ourselves.' – **KJ**

'I wanted to be a professional too much. Emotionally the knockbacks affected me, while Gavin still had the same love and enjoyment after his knockbacks I took them personally and changed the way I played slightly to impress the decision makers. My view on my past was that I invested everything to make it as a professional, but my ill treatment affected me, so I fell out of love with the professional game.

'After hustling my way into football, I found it difficult when I was released from my contract. I tried to get another club, but I wasn't serious about it, it was just the only way I knew to make money. I went from being super fit and super keen to being a passenger in the game. I was emotionally drained. During the conversations we had while writing this chapter Gavin said that he believed I had been affected because I had invested everything in becoming a professional footballer and not a football player. He was partly right; I am hungry to be at the top of whatever I do. Gavin and Craig wanted to be professionals, but they were willing to wait for the opportunity whereas I wasn't, so I created the opportunities that helped me get signed. It's a toughie because maybe if I hadn't got signed when I did, I would have developed a more resilient identity like Craig and Gavin did.' – **KG**

Players we admired

'Dean MacDonald's feet were fire! He came through the Arsenal academy and went on to play for Ipswich Town and Gillingham. The things he could do with a ball were out of this world. Like the top Brazilians he would beat skilled players casually. On top of that he had a great first touch and could use his weaker foot to a good standard.

'James Allen's self-belief and his ability to deliver on it were insane! I remember when I was on trial at West Ham having a kick about on the indoor AstroTurf, James must have beaten about three players while talking to them at the same time. He then approached the goal keeper, Billy McMahon, dummied him, sat him down on the floor and then said, "one-two", kicked the ball off Billy's chest, got it back again and scored.

'Dwight Gayle's finishing was sublime. He was at the point in his career where he was trying to get back into professional football after his days as a kid at Arsenal and non-league football. We were both at Dagenham and Redbridge. I was starting for the first team while Dwight was struggling to get into the first team. I was thinking, "This guy is better than me at finishing, it wasn't even close and I'm playing ahead of him". His finishing was phenomenal; we would go out before training with a bag of balls to do finishing and I would tell him to use his left foot, expecting him to struggle because I was struggling, so we could both work on our weaker foot together, but he was just slamming the ball into the net with his weaker foot. In a worst-case scenario he would come off the bench for the last 30 minutes of games at Dagenham. I would gladly have come off for him.' – **GT**

'I had always known Rohan Rickets was good from his days at Arsenal, but when he was at Wolverhampton Wanderers, he showed me how good he was. There was a season when I was at Sheffield Wednesday where we played Wolves four times as we went to the same pre-season tournament. He played alongside Paul Ince who was the holding midfielder which allowed him to push forward to create. In one of the games, the ref blew the whistle for kick-off, Rohan got the ball, ran towards me, threw two step-overs and was gone in a flash, while I was left stranded. We still laugh about that moment to this day. He was a good passer and good dribbler, one of the best players I have played against.

'Jason Koumas was one of the most talented players I have ever played against. He had great technique when stroking a ball, made great decisions and was quick. A dangerous combination of skills to play against, trust me, I know. Jason was a great player that didn't like all the rubbish that came with the game, he just wanted to play football and I think this prevented him from achieving the career his talent deserved.

'Frazer Toms was a youth player at Charlton that never made it through, but that boy's Cruyff Turn was best I've ever seen. In the heat of a competitive game against top level opponents when it was all going at a hundred miles an hour Frazer would perform a Cruyff Turn and kill the game's erratic pace.

'At Chelsea I was spoilt for players to learn from. Seeing Leon Knight do things in training or in a game on a regular basis was a pleasure, the kid was phenomenal. I can't pick out any one thing in particular; everything was top notch.

'Mbark Bousaffa could take any ball on the bounce, moving sharply and comfortably with possession. Ranieri's last year at Chelsea was his last year too as he wasn't offered another deal. If he'd had one more year, he would have flourished under Mourinho.

'What Juan Sebastian Veron could do with a ball was amazing. People criticise Veron's performances in England, but it was because he didn't like the culture and playing against smaller teams that wanted to rattle you didn't really interest him. Technically he was able to do anything, putting the ball where he wanted when shooting or passing and I'm not talking about the basic stuff either. When Glen Johnson came to Chelsea he was very good, he had everything: pace, strength, he could read the game and was comfortable in possession but Mourinho broke him in two. Claudio Ranieiri was different from Mourinho. For starters, he didn't speak English unless he really wanted to and didn't really familiarise himself with people, but Mourinho had the club on a different structure. Mourinho doesn't like egotistical players; he didn't like Adrian Mutu or Glen Johnson, anybody that was flashy and extravagant. Johnno turning up in a Porsche one day, another car the next day and so on was not to Mourinho's liking so he would put Johnno on the spot in training by asking him to do demonstrations. Under the pressure Johnno crumbled, he was not the same player after two and a half weeks of pre-season under Mourinho. When Ranieri bought Johnno, he played every game but when Mourinho came there were times he wasn't even in the squad! Mentally he was broken. Mourinho didn't say anything to break Johnno, but the experience he created for him was not a good one.

'Joe Cole was my favourite English player, watching him on the come up and then being at the same club when I was at Chelsea was enjoyable to say the least. It was a shame he let his superstition get the best of him. He also worried too much about stuff like what was being written about him in the papers. His heart was too big; if he'd had the mentality of Jermaine Defoe he would have been alright. For example, when he came to Chelsea it wasn't going too well at the beginning, so to recapture the great form of his younger years he tried to recreate how he looked back then. He regrew his hair and started wearing Adidas Copa Mundial football boots again. During this period, I remember him ruining William Gallas in a one-on-one training session. If he'd had the right mentality he would have been one of the icons of English football because his talent was off the charts. Mourinho was a huge fan of Joe. When he was playing for England and they were knocked out of the European Championships he was given a break, like all the other players in international tournaments, before returning to club football. He came straight back into training after one day. Mourinho told him that he shouldn't be in and that he should be resting, Joe told him, "I'm good and ready to train." The kid loved football. Gallas was not his only victim, he did so many things to people that Mourinho would stop the session and say "This is football!" – **CR**

'Erhan Oztumer was a player that could take the game by the scruff of the neck. As a player/coach for Dulwich Hamlet I got the chance to experience Erhan in two different ways. Playing alongside him or watching from the sides, he gave you the reassurance that he could provide the winner or get us out of a hole at any moment. He is technically gifted and made the right decisions while carrying the pressure of being the team's saviour from a young age.

'I can only echo Craig's views on Frazer's Cruyff Turns; he would change the whole wave of the game within that moment.

'I remember Jermaine Defoe coming back from Lilleshall to Charlton, I didn't know who he was at the time and he was on the bench for one of our youth team games against Crystal Palace. I was thinking, "hang on a second, this isn't right! A young kid three years younger than us who hasn't been around just turns up and gets on the bench." Jon Fortune then told me that he was unbelievable. They were from the same area and Jon knew all about young Jermaine, who had previously played for the well-known Senrab FC. Jermaine came off the bench that game for the last 30 minutes and scored a hat-trick!

'When John Barnes was approaching the end of his career, he transitioned into a centre midfielder and came to Charlton. He used to drop me home now and again and all he spoke about was football. He lived the game and couldn't understand why the younger kids didn't want to speak about football all the time too. He marshalled (controlled) the training games; he was like a puppet master and had the whole team on strings while dictating the play. A technical leader by a country mile.

'In youth football I played against Arsenal's Paolo Vernazza, Ashley Cole and other top players but Craig Bellamy in youth football was phenomenal. He was quick, worked hard and had an all-rounded game. There were players that had the sharpness of Craig and similar ability, but he played with a maturity beyond his years. He was direct and knew how to make the most of his talent.' – **KJ**

From youth team to first team as a professional I would look to come short and look good on the ball, but when I went into non-league I realised that it's good to get on the ball and keep the game ticking. I learnt this lesson too late. I prioritised linking up play and playing through balls over running in behind to score goals, but at the end of the day when people judge me the question will be: how many goals did I score? I was an unselfish player, I was too unselfish. Look at Jermaine Defoe, he gets the ball, he turns, and he shoots. No one told me I had to be more selfish, no one told me to direct my game towards scoring more goals. It was an epiphany that came too late in my mind. In fact, I learnt how to run in behind when I was on the bench for QPR and we were playing against Blackburn in the FA Cup. Craig Bellamy was playing and his run ins behind were unbelievable. No one had got past our centre back Danny Shittu for six months, during this game he didn't know what to do or where he was. I was watching the game wondering how on earth Bellamy got onto the end of every ball and that's how I learnt to run in behind. Surely, I should have been taught that, but I had to learn this myself at 22 years old.

—**Stefan Moore**
former Aston Villa and England international

'I would say the best of all was Kieran Dyer. During his youth team days, he was playing for Ipswich Town and I was at Charlton. We beat them five nil and he was unbelievable! I don't understand how someone could have been so good for their team and still lose five nil, that tells you a lot about Kieran. He was everywhere, playing as a centre midfielder but running into the position of the number 10, 11 and 7. Kieran was gliding past players, speeding the game up, slowing it down and creating chances; the problem was that his teammates couldn't convert them.' – **KJ**

'Lionel Morgan is a well-known player on the football circuit; unfortunately he had to retire at 21 due to injury. Before retirement, Lionel played for England youth teams, Wimbledon FC and he also came close to joining Tottenham as a teenager but failed the medical. Lionel was a great player; he ghosted past players like they weren't there. I remember Craig talking about Lionel after he'd had an off-season kick about against him and my teammates getting scared before the game like they usually did every time we faced a super talent. They had lost the game in their minds before it had even begun. I went into the game determined to come out on top because I have always found extra motivation when I'm facing the best. Although I was playing centre midfield and Lionel was on the left wing I knew our paths would cross during the game and they did.

'Lionel was running rings around my teammates and on one of his runs he decided to cut inside into my territory. I thought, "Now I'm going to show my teammates how to deal with him." He touched the ball too far away for me to intercept but he was still close enough for me to get the better of him. BANG! I invested everything into a shoulder barge. I gave more than I needed to because apart from intending to knock him off balance and gain possession, I wanted to send him a message about what would happen every time he entered a dual with me. My plan failed as my barge only knocked him off balance, which he regained quickly and ran off with the ball. I was one of the stronger ones in my age group so that had never happened before, things would either go my way or I would concede a foul. Lionel had skill, speed, strength and intelligence.

'Joe Cole was a top talent; I had the pleasure of watching him train when I was at West Ham and got to witness him even closer as I had to man-mark him in the FA Youth Cup. I didn't fall victim to his skills, in fact many said I marked him out of the game, but he lost me twice with two great changes of speed and direction, one leading to an assist, to a game that was already settled. Joe jumped from first gear to fifth gear with ease.

'Jermaine Defoe's mindset was unbelievable; he went into games with a mission – goals. We were told to think about the team, but Defoe had his own mission. If we had won and he hadn't scored he wasn't happy, if we had lost and he had scored, he would be content. He had a great balance of team and personal objectives while the rest of the players only thought about the team. That was one of the reasons he had a great career. I heard Harry Redknapp asking coaches about our games and who had scored. Defoe's name would be mentioned among the goal scorers regularly.

'When Leon Britton came to West Ham, we didn't know much about him. After leaving Lilleshall, Leon went looking for a new club because he thought opportunities to get to the first team at Arsenal, the club he was signed to, were limited. He had a contract offer on the table from Arsenal, but he turned it down in favour of joining a club where he believed there would be more of a pathway towards the first team. Britton also turned down offers from Aston Villa and Chelsea before signing for West Ham. He signed at the same time as Defoe, so his signing was drowned out by the attention placed on the Defoe transfer until his first keep ball session. Everyone was full of the highest praise for Britton. I remember Izzy Iriekpen hollering, "Oh my God! Have you seen Brittzy play? The kid is unbelievable!"

'Glen Johnson was about two years younger than me at West Ham but played up in my age group. Like Craig said, he was quick, strong, composed in possession, and in the tackle. He was a centre back in our youth team days and he had everything.' – **KG**

Johan Cruyff was one of my heroes as a youngster because of his style of play, smooth flowing movement and comfort on the ball. He was the spearhead of the Total Football style played by the Holland national team. I will always remember Cruyff from the 1974 World Cup where the world witnessed the Cruyff Turn for the first time on the biggest stage in world football.

It was the 1983/84 season, the 19th of October 1983, Tottenham versus Feyenoord in the UEFA Cup at White Hart Lane, the crowd in excess of 35,000. This game was about the master versus the young genius, Johan Cruyff versus Glenn Hoddle going head to head in midfield. Hoddle was brilliant in the first half, playing a part in all our goals, which saw us leading 4-0 at half time. There was an element of disappointment in the crowd and among the Spurs players, myself very much included, because Cruyff hardly got on the ball. It was a buzz for us to be playing against him and he was disappointing.

In the second half, the ball was played towards Cruyff but it was underhit, giving the defender belief that he could intercept. Cruyff's fake movement towards the ball encouraged the defender to go to ground in a mistimed attempt to intercept. Cruyff moved away in the opposite direction, the ball met him there and with a quick change of pace he ran towards the Tottenham goal, playing a one-two pass around one player then he came up against me. Just inside the eighteen-yard box, to our right, he shifted the ball towards the centre of the goal and – Bang! I dived in with an attempted block to his shot but was unable to stop the low drive he smashed into the net.

Despite his poor performance in the first half, he had a presence about him that seemed to grow as the second half progressed, which led to him running the game, dictating as well as scoring one of Feyenoord's two second-half goals. I was 21 at the time and Cruyff was 36. In the second half he certainly didn't play like someone 36 years old. He glided around the pitch and kept the ball effortlessly with crisp passing and brilliant use of his body to protect the ball when he was challenged.

—**Gary Stevens**
former Tottenham and England international

Lianne and Leanne

'She always has a ball!' I said. I was walking with Craig from his house to Kevin James' house. 'Who?' I described the little girl I was talking about.

'Oh, that's Lianne,' Craig said casually. He was already aware of Lianne's passion for the game. Craig and Kevin lived a two-minute walk away from each other. The road splitting their road in two was the road Lianne lived on. Over the years that we four boys met up to play football or socialise, we would see Lianne walking with her mum and a ball.

Lianne's hours of investment with the boys on the street helped her to hone her skills and become an international footballer. She went from the streets of Bellingham to playing for the Arsenal Ladies' first team at 14, scoring on her debut, and then playing for the England Women's first team at 16. From 2006 to 2008 Lianne scored 91 goals in 77 games for Arsenal and is second on their goal-scoring hall of fame with 139 goals. Her environment involved a group of people who challenged her physically and socially, preparing her for the challenges ahead.

I grew up in a football-obsessed family, going to my dad's games from six months old. I would play football with the boys on the street seven-plus hours per day, only stopping when my mum called me in because it was dark. Playing football with boys was key for my development because apart from the hours invested in developing my skills, I was also developing a thick skin so I could ignore what others thought of a girl playing football. I always had a ball under my arm, I just wanted to play football, I didn't think about being a girl or the only girl.

—**Lianne Sanderson**
former Arsenal Ladies and England striker

It was the summer of 2013 and I was tired after a long day of fulfilling my best man duties at my brother Marvin's wedding. It was about 10:00 pm and the wedding reception was still going on, so I stepped out into the garden of the Bromley Court hotel and saw a young lady with a ball at her feet. After being surprised for a few moments that someone had brought a football to a wedding, I asked the usual, 'Hey, can I have a kick?' The lady passed me the ball. I took a few touches, passed it back to her and asked her name. 'My name's Leanne.'

We had a brief exchange about who she knew at the wedding, football and her local area. I couldn't believe I had met someone with a similar name to Lianne, who was also mixed race, from Bellingham (a five to ten-minute walk from Lianne's house), who loved football, carried a ball with her to places, communicated with the same sense of confidence about herself and was also a professional footballer.

I grew up playing football on the estate with friends or my brother. After a couple of years my friends moved away and my brother was more interested in his Xbox so I'd play by myself. I worked on strengthening my weaker foot and improving my first touch. I'd repeatedly try to beat my kick ups record, practised sharp turns and skills that I'd learnt at my Brazilian Soccer School Futból dã Sàlao.

—**Leanne Cowan**
Millwall Ladies FC defender

Four boys from Bellingham used the power of the group to create an environment to support their dream. One girl from Bellingham used the conditions created by the group she played with to develop into an international footballer, and another made it by herself.

The environment is not one thing; it is made up of many things which combine in different ways. Gavin, Craig, Kevin and I created an environment of high expectation, pressure, consistency and commitment. Lianne's environment was one she used to develop her physical skills, unconscious competence and resilience. Leanne created her own environment; she was the environment. After training with Futból dã Sàlao, she dedicated 15 to 20 hours per week to training by herself. She was her own critic, she set her own standards, her own pressure and committed to the cause in her drive to succeed.

Players from England, or anywhere else in the world, who want to get into the professional game or who want to know how they can last longer in the professional game have access to different environments. They may not have a group of friends or teammates that have the same desire and commitment, but they can use the group for their own development and if that fails, look inwards. There is no wrong or right way.

Questions to assess your group

- Does my group challenge me when I do not perform well, strategically hide from doing extra work, or hide from getting the ball?
- Is the group brave enough to challenge me?
- Is the group aware of the requirements needed to progress?
- Are they as committed as me? If not, where can I find another group to train with? If they are more committed,

are you working on improving your commitment or are you being dependant on the group? Commitment means turning up and doing whatever it takes to improve.

These questions are also important when assessing yourself, especially when there is no group.

At the end of the day...

Yes, it's an old footballing cliché, but quite appropriate as I draw this to a close. Because, at the end of the day, I believe that it is possible for everyone to have a great experience in football, no matter their background or culture. The key to everything is education. Those in charge of the welfare of players: coaches and staff need to educate themselves about the latest research in how thoughts and feelings affect performance. Parents and friends of players need to understand the pressures and emotions involved in playing the game at any level, including the very top. Being a big-name player does not mean you are immune to problems or suddenly have no feelings. On the contrary, the pressures of high-level football are immense and can lead to a whole raft of specific issues for those involved.

Players can do a lot to educate themselves. As I mentioned before, if you don't have the right people around to encourage and support you, then take on that role yourself. Invest in self-development, learn how your mind works and study the effects emotions can have on performance. Being aware is more than half the battle.

I hope the insights from those directly involved in this beautiful game of ours have helped open your eyes to the value of thinking skills and how someone's psycho-emotional state can affect their performance and their life. Soccology is my way of spreading the word; if it makes even one player, coach or parent think more deeply about how they can be the best version of themselves and encourage others to do the same, then this book will have done its job.

ACKNOWLEDGEMENTS

I would like to thank all the contributors for taking the time out to share part of themselves.

Maggie Albrecht for assistance in explaining Neuro-Logical Levels.

Crystal Mahey-Morgan and Jason Morgan at my publisher OWN IT! for their belief in this book and the collaborative nature in which we work.

Fiona Cameron Lister for her great work in editing this book.

James Nunn for the cover illustration and design.

Chanelle Newman for always being on hand to give advice.

Steve Payne and John Thompson for being the best teachers I have ever had. You both give great information, while being captivating. When it comes to engagement, you guys are kings!

Kelly, a man who gave up his time to manage kids from the streets of New Cross. The attention you gave to all those little boys, myself included, was invaluable. You played a key role in the lives of many young professionals that came out of New Cross and Moonshot FC.

Craig Rocastle, Kevin James and Gavin Tomlin. Without you guys, I had no chance of getting into professional football.

My teammates who passed away during their careers Pierre Bolangi, Richard Butcher and to my former manager that passed away Keith Alexander.

ABOUT THE AUTHOR

Kevin George is a Human Performance Consultant and founder of The Vivo Team. He spent eight years as a professional footballer, for notable clubs such as West Ham United and Charlton Athletic FC. After retiring as a professional footballer, Kevin used his experience and insight to develop *SOCCOLOGY*, a human performance programme that has been widely endorsed by key footballing and sports figures around the world.

Kevin regularly works with prisons on conflict resolution and the *SOCCOLOGY* programme has been delivered across all Premier League football clubs. He delivers emotional literacy programmes all over the world, helping attendees to be a better version of themselves both personally and professionally.

His work has been published internationally, including by the British Council, and has been translated into seven different languages. He is also a sought after international public speaker committed to improving the experiences of others. Kevin's philanthropic work has led to him sitting on a host of advisory boards. He is a member of Kick it Out's Professional Player's Guidance Group and the Professional Footballers' Association.

Kevin is a passionate advocate for how understanding human behaviour can have a significant impact on decision making both on and off the pitch.

Photo: Steve Bridge

Photo: Steve Bridge

ABOUT OWN IT!

OWN IT! is a storytelling lifestyle brand, sharing stories across books, music, fashion and film. At the heart of everything we do is a desire to share, empower, celebrate and inspire. Whether it's through multi-media digital books, print books, music or film, OWN IT! releases original and authentic stories told in creative new ways.

WWW.OWNIT.LONDON
@OWNITLDN